NEW DIRECTIONS
FOR
PHILANTHROPIC
FUNDRAISING

Robert E. Fogal
Ohio Presbyterian Retirement Services Foundation;
formerly of the Indiana University Center on Philanthropy
EDITOR-IN-CHIEF

WOMEN AS DONORS, WOMEN AS PHILANTHROPISTS

Abbie J. von Schlegell
Barnes & Roche, Inc.
Joan M. Fisher
B'nai B'rith Women
EDITORS

NUMBER 2, WINTER 1993

WOMEN AS DONORS, WOMEN AS PHILANTHROPISTS
Abbie J. von Schlegell, Joan M. Fisher (eds.)
New Directions for Philanthropic Fundraising, No. 2, Winter 1993
Robert E. Fogal, Editor-in-Chief

Microfilm copies of issues and articles are available in 16 mm and 35 mm, as well as microfiche in 105 mm, through University Microfilms Inc., 300 North Zeeb Road, Ann Arbor, Michigan 48106-1346.

ISSN 1072-172X   ISBN 1-55542-713-8

NEW DIRECTIONS FOR PHILANTHROPIC FUNDRAISING is part of The Jossey-Bass Nonprofit Sector Series and is published quarterly by Jossey-Bass Inc., Publishers, 350 Sansome Street, San Francisco, California 94104-1310.

SUBSCRIPTIONS: Please see Ordering Information at back of book.

EDITORIAL CORRESPONDENCE should be sent to Robert E. Fogal, Ohio Presbyterian Retirement Services Foundation, OMNI Plaza, 4502 Darrow Rd., Rte. 91, Stow, OH 44224-1887.

Manufactured in the United States of America. Nearly all Jossey-Bass books, jackets, and periodicals are printed on recycled paper that contains at least 50 percent recycled waste, including 10 percent postconsumer waste. Many of our materials are also printed with vegetable-based ink; during the printing process these inks emit fewer volatile organic compounds (VOCs) than petroleum-based inks. VOCs contribute to the formation of smog.

Contents

Editors' Notes

WOMEN AS DONORS, WOMEN AS PHILANTHROPISTS is a collection of practical discussions about the ways development officers can effectively employ the behaviors and preferences of women in programs that center on women donors and philanthropists. While these discussions emphasize fundraising work completed in higher education, they include information about development activity in other nonprofit arenas as well. Readers should view all these essays about the growing awareness of women donors, start-up programs for women donors and potential donors, and the measurable successes of programs for women donors as first steps in a discourse. Each chapter uncovers an agenda for further research and, we think, will assist in furthering women's influence in philanthropy. However, each author has also recognized how often empirical or quantitative evidence to validate his or her claims and conclusions was simply unavailable, showing that development officers must continue to seek both historic and current examples of effective philanthropy by women and to encourage their contemporaries to seek creative ways to express that philanthropy.

We hope the chapters in this volume will be a catalyst first for awareness and discussion and subsequently for changes in attitudes among professional fundraisers and women donors. By applying the rationales, suggestions, and techniques that are proposed by the different authors, institutions can strengthen their own development programs and encourage women donors and potential women philanthropists to have a greater impact than they do now.

Women as Donors, Women as Philanthropists is organized around several broad themes. The first theme is the current state of studies in women's philanthropy. In Chapter One, Ann E. Kaplan and M. Joanne Hayes establish a context in which the study of women

NEW DIRECTIONS FOR PHILANTHROPIC FUNDRAISING, NO. 2, WINTER 1993 © JOSSEY-BASS PUBLISHERS

philanthropists can be set and an approach to that study. The discussion also suggests how much statistical research on this issue has yet to be done. Sondra C. Shaw, in Chapter Two, and Paula J. Faust and H. Sargent Whittier, Jr., in Chapter Three, discuss issues of communication, marketing style, and professional expectations and suggest that knowing about women's philanthropic behavior and acting upon that information may be more complicated than development officers have typically assumed. The second theme is the analysis of specific fundraising programs. In Chapters Four, Five, Six, and Seven, development officers Dyan Sublett, Kaye Ferguson-Patton, Ronald A. Joyce, Tracy West Barlok, and Martha A. Taylor describe aspects of program applications in their own institutions. These programs aim to give women in philanthropy special attention and already appear to be making some positive difference in fundraising results. The third and final theme focuses on philanthropic programs that have used a new paradigm about women and their philanthropic potential and have succeeded because of that new approach. Chapter Eight, by Susan Church and Carol Mollner, describes the strengths and goals of women's philanthropic foundations. Chapter Nine, by Karen D. Stone, Susan F. Rice, and Judith C. Angel, focuses on women's philanthropy in the political process. And in Chapter Ten, Nicki Newman Tanner and Peter Ramsey describe a successful capital campaign. The final chapter reviews the growing number of programs that support many of the suggestions made by the authors of this volume, and the Selected Bibliography includes some women's foundations and other special sources in addition to books, articles, reports, and newsletters.

In this volume, the chapter authors often distinguish donors from philanthropists. Women's transition or evolution from donors to philanthropists can take place over time through not only women's acquisition of assets and wealth being applied to gift giving but also through women's practiced decision making and charity and through a change in both the recognition and impact of a gift. While many women can be and are donors, a woman becomes a philanthropist only after significant charitable gift giving with a pattern of consistent, intense effect on a cause or project. The amount of money given is not the criteria, but rather the effect of the gift on the cause, institution, or project. That is, a charitable act becomes philanthropic when the anticipated (or even unexpected) effect of the gift is to reach multitudes of humankind rather than just one individual.

We have appreciated the opportunity to meet and work with the chapter authors—both volunteer and professional development officers—who through their own growing awareness of the issues, are establishing the kinds of connections among themselves that will enable them to further support and encourage women in every form of philanthropy. As coeditors we are particularly grateful to the Center on Women in Philanthropy at the University of Wisconsin and the Johnson Foundation for sponsoring the conference "Women and Philanthropy" in 1992 at Wingspread in Racine, Wisconsin, and to the National Council for Research on Women for hosting the conference "Funding Women" in 1993, where women of diverse backgrounds developed national agendas for research about and action for women in philanthropy. Our authors have augmented the "Funding Women" agendas with questions raised by their own endeavors with women donors. While identifying numerous topics that methodical research might validate, the authors of this volume also bring optimism and enthusiasm to their emerging work with women donors and philanthropists. Each author is aware that studies about women's philanthropic achievements merit further attention as does continuing evaluation of the programs described here and their encouragement of philanthropic behavior.

We would like to thank Carol Lazerik, Muriel Feldman Rothstein, Katharine Hickey, and Susan Tomchin for their reading and valuable comments about these chapters. Denise Nelson, Dora Oldes, and Sara Walter provided valuable production assistance in the early stages. Jing Lyman of Stanford first prompted the examination of this important subject over twenty years ago—how right she was to place an emphasis on women's giving. Gretchen von Schlegell pitched in at the last moment to help us with the final chapter—we thank her. Barnes & Roche, Inc., has shown tremendous patience and generosity in allowing Abbie J. von Schlegell to commit the necessary time to this important project. The support staff at Barnes & Roche were exemplary in their efforts to produce the final manuscript and to keep us all connected when our demanding travel schedules made communication challenging. Finally, we want to acknowledge Jossey-Bass and the Indiana University Center on Philanthropy for encouraging attention to this issue—attention we believe is long overdue.

Abbie J. von Schlegell,
Joan M. Fisher
Editors

ABBIE J. VON SCHLEGELL *is senior vice president of Barnes & Roche, Inc., a national firm specializing in institutional advancement consulting and executive search services. She assisted in founding the Center for Research on Women (now the Institute for Research on Women and Gender) at Stanford University.*

JOAN M. FISHER *is an association executive with B'nai B'rith Women in Washington, D.C., and managing partner of James L. Fisher, Ltd., a consulting firm that advises institutions of higher education on leadership, governance, management, and philanthropy.*

A summary of the current research about women as donors to nonprofit organizations reveals what that research does and does not say about the attributes and potential of women as donors and women as philanthropists.

1

What we know about women as donors

Ann E. Kaplan, M. Joanne Hayes

RECENTLY, there has been a surge of interest in the role women play as donors to nonprofits. Amid the speculation about possible causes of this heightened interest, one reason stands out as the most plausible. That reason is money. Fundraisers think that more and more women will be in control of charitable dollars. However, reliable empirical data that distinguish between the characteristics of male and female donors are scarce. One pattern that does emerge from a review of the research on charitable giving is that the major reason why any particular population segment—such as women, blacks, or Hispanics—gives or does not give is not necessarily to be found in its culture, psychology, or sex. Instead, individual giving is strongly correlated with the answers to these three questions: Does the person think he or she can afford to give? Does the person know and value the organization? Was the person asked to give?

NEW DIRECTIONS FOR PHILANTHROPIC FUNDRAISING, NO. 2, WINTER 1993 © JOSSEY-BASS PUBLISHERS

Why do women give?

The results of some specific fundraising campaigns, however, suggest that certain relationships and recognition might be of special importance to women donors.

The experience of women's colleges

Wellesley, a prestigious women's college in Massachusetts, received much attention when it had the highest level of per student alumni giving among all colleges and universities for the 1989–90 fiscal year. Bryn Mawr, another women's college, ranked third. Moreover, women's colleges accounted for five of the top eleven colleges in per student alumni contributions that year (Council for Aid to Education, 1991). The following year, the trend was similar. Wellesley still ranked first, and half of the top twelve colleges were women's colleges (Council for Aid to Education, 1992).

Can fundraisers generalize from alumni giving to giving from other donors? Historically, persons between the ages of thirty-five and sixty-four have been the most generous donors to nonprofits. Many of the prestigious coed colleges were once all male, and their alumni donors within the primary donor age range are still likely to be men, even though the schools currently enroll women. Thus, if women's colleges rely on a female donor base for alumnae giving while coeducational colleges rely primarily on male donors, fundraising data from women's colleges may reveal something about sex differences in general giving patterns.

Of course, spouses may bear some responsibility for a family's charitable giving to any college, and that influence would render the alumni donor profile somewhat more complex than it appears at first glance. Moreover, though colleges in general get a substantial amount of support (26 percent) from alumni, 42 percent of their support comes from corporations and foundations (Council for Aid to Education, 1992). Among the top forty institutions that received half the corporate dollars to higher education and among the top thirty-seven schools receiving half the foundation grants to higher education, there is not a single women's college (McMillen, 1991, pp. 21, 23).

Further, it has been argued that alumnae of prestigious women's colleges are not typical donors and therefore it is not correct to generalize from their behavior to the behavior of typical U.S. women. For one thing, prestigious women's college alumnae are wealthier than other women. Many are from relatively affluent households, and after graduating, they tend to fare better in earnings than the average U.S. woman of the same age. If they marry, their husbands also have more financial resources than the average U.S. man. The other distinguishing characteristic of these alumnae is that, presumably, they are relatively well educated. In addition, though many of the top women's colleges have need-blind admissions policies and strive for racial and cultural diversity, overall they still attract and enroll a select population. Their alumnae pool cannot be described as representative of the country as a whole. These colleges, though they would promote their student populations as "diverse," would probably not refer to them as "average." And certainly, in the aggregate, the population on these campuses does not come from households with anything near average income levels.

Thus, the success of women's colleges in raising alumnae dollars can be attributed in part to the special characteristics of the alumnae. However, these particular special qualities should describe men in selective colleges also, and so these qualities do not explain why Wellesley, for example, did better in per student alumni giving than Harvard, Yale, and Princeton. Wellesley's involvement in a major capital campaign at the time helped, of course, but that campaign was carefully orchestrated, emphasizing women's unique motives for giving (see Chapter Ten).

Recognition versus relationships

Those who are experts at soliciting gifts from women say that, while men cherish recognition and status, women want to be involved with organizations to which they contribute money. They value relationships with organizations to which they contribute and aspire to understand these organizations and even to help shape their programs. However, studies on giving have repeatedly shown a relationship between giving and volunteering among both men and women. Both sexes give more when they are involved with an organization and understand what it is doing.

Giving to higher education and giving to religion

The donor trait of giving to organizations in which the donor is personally involved explains why colleges and universities are such successful fundraisers in general. They have at least four years to cultivate relationships with prospective donors. Indeed, most personal contributions go to either higher education or religious institutions. In the latter case, the relationship between donor and donee is not only personal, it may be also be described as spiritual.

That women who attend women's colleges may be particularly devoted to those colleges does not mean that men who are similarly devoted to specific institutions are not motivated by that devotion in their giving. It also does not mean that women would universally eschew prestige and recognition in exchange for their monetary contributions if such recognition were offered.

Interviews with wealthy women

Major donors are idiosyncratic. Much of the research about giving by women focuses upon interviews with wealthy women, and it underscores the diversity of responses wealthy women have to the act of giving money. The assumption that some universal quality exists in the female donor may be based upon isolated examples rather than empirical data. When women have independent control of healthy incomes or large fortunes, is their giving behavior similar to or different from the behavior of their male counterparts? There is no evidence either way.

What empirical research shows

The empirical research currently available falls into four major categories: estate tax return data and projections, household surveys, consumer and demographic research, and research about women in the foundation world. Although some of this research shows a correlation between sex differences and behavioral differences, users of the research should remember that such correlations do not necessarily mean there are cause-and-effect relationships between the variables. It is one thing to prove that two factors are related to each other; it is another thing entirely to prove that one caused the other.

Estate giving

For example, at death, significantly more women (27 percent) than men (15 percent) leave bequests to charity, and in estates worth $5 million or more, nearly 48 percent of female decedents make a charitable bequest compared to 35 percent of male decedents (Johnson and Rosenfeld, 1991, p. 30). This certainly is a sex difference, but it is not necessarily a difference caused by gender. Because married women outlive married men, it may be that the men left their estates to their wives, who later made a charitable bequest. Indeed, there is a tax advantage to leaving a bequest to a charity rather than to a son or daughter, but there is no tax advantage to leaving money to charity rather than one's spouse. Thus, the sex difference observed in estate giving could be a difference in longevity, which is itself correlated with, but not necessarily caused by, gender.

Actually, among those decedents who leave a charitable bequest, women tend to give the same percent of their net worth regardless of the size of their estates. By contrast, men give larger proportions of larger estates; so while women are more likely to leave charitable bequests, men with the largest estates give more than women with estates of the same size. Indeed, the annual dollar value of charitable bequests by men exceeds that of women's bequests (Johnson and Rosenfeld, 1991, p. 30).

Thus, depending upon the variable examined, women can be made to look more generous or less generous than men in their willed giving. But in fact, marital status is probably more significant in predicting willed giving than is sex (Johnson and Rosenfeld, 1991, p. 31).

Household surveys

Marital status also complicates responses to household surveys about giving. In a recent survey on giving and volunteering in the United States, conducted by the Independent Sector for the Gallup Organization, female respondents reported giving a lower proportion of household income than did male respondents. What is perplexing, though, is that this difference is virtually entirely due to the reporting of married respondents (see Figure 1.1). Single, separated, divorced, and widowed respondents reported that their

Figure 1.1. Household Giving as a Percentage of Income by Marital Status and Sex

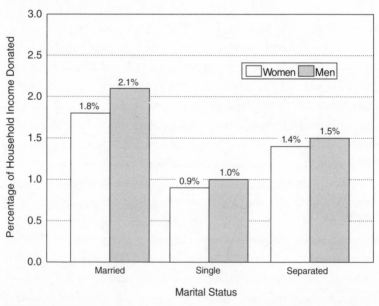

Adapted from Hodgkinson, Weitzman, Noga, and Gorski, 1992, pp. 97, 100, 103.

households gave about the same percentage of income regardless of the sex of the respondent. Only in households with married respondents, where household giving should be identical whether the husband or the wife reports it, did men and women report different giving levels. We have speculated about the reasons for this difference. For example, when women live alone, they may be more aware of how much the household gives than when they are married, because single women have to account for only their own giving. Or maybe married men exaggerate household-giving levels. Or it could actually be the case that married women give less and assume their husbands give the way they do. Whatever the reason for the difference in reporting, it is a small difference, only about three-tenths of a percent. So it is hard to imagine why the results of this study and previous giving and volunteering surveys have been used to support the contention that women give less than men. Not only is the difference very small, it is likely to be a reporting difference. The most definitive thing one can say about the results is that women say their households give a little less than men say.

Are there differences in giving between men and women of different races? When studies of discrete racial groups are controlled for income, there is once again little variation between women's and men's giving. In the Independent Sector/Gallup survey, Hispanic men reported the lowest and white men the highest levels of household giving as a percentage of income. Within each race, there were only small differences between what men reported and what women reported about household giving. The largest difference—four-tenths of one percent—occurred in Hispanic households, where women reported more giving than men (see Figure 1.2).

Women of color

One earlier survey (Carson, 1987) asked women about their personal as opposed to household giving. The percentage of respondents who said they did not make a gift was nearly the same (about 18 percent) for both black and white women (pp. 12–13). The same

Figure 1.2. Household Giving as a Percentage of Income by Race and Sex

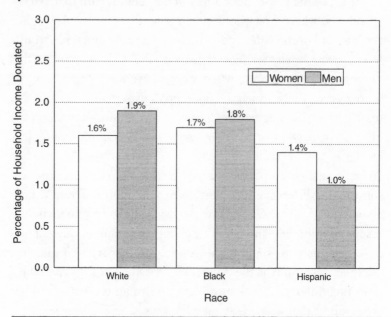

Adapted from Hodgkinson, Weitzman, Noga, and Gorski, 1992, pp. 97, 100, 103.

survey uncovered other details of note. For example, more unemployed than employed white women in the study made gifts, though unemployed white women made more small gifts than their employed counterparts. Among black women, however, more employed than unemployed respondents made gifts, and not being employed or earning very little money depressed giving frequency more in black women than in white women (see Figures 1.3 and 1.4). Also, when controlled for income, black and white women reported nearly identical frequencies of giving except in the middle range of income, where black women gave more frequently (see Figure 1.5).

Race, gender, and being asked to give

The Independent Sector/Gallup survey highlighted another factor about the giving patterns of blacks and Hispanics, pointing out that

Figure 1.3. Percentage of Women Who Did *Not* Contribute by Race and Employment Status

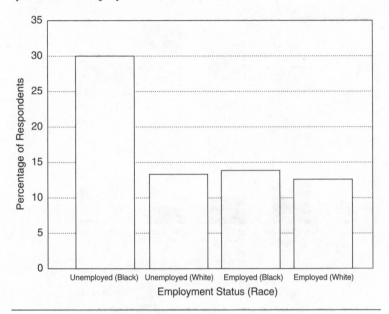

Adapted from Carson, 1987, pp. 12–13.

blacks and Hispanics "are not asked to give at the same rate as the rest of the population. . . . Findings clearly show that . . . these groups are even more likely to give when asked than other groups in the population" (Hodgkinson, Weitzman, Noga, and Gorski, 1992, p. 210). White respondents were only slightly more likely to give when asked as when not asked. Whereas, black or Hispanic respondents were closer to 2.5 times as likely to give when asked.

Asking women to give

The effect of asking was not much different for women than men in the Independent Sector/Gallup survey, and surveyed women actually reported that they were slightly more likely to be asked for contributions than men reported they were. Yet, the relationship between being asked and giving lends some support to professionals' opinions about women's giving. Development professionals at

Figure 1.4. Percentage of Women Who Contributed by Race and Employment Status

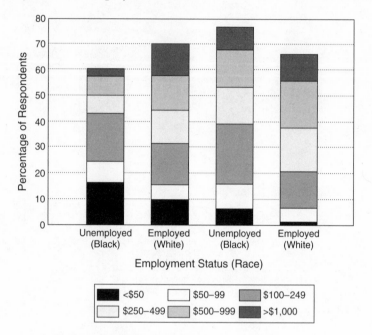

Source: Adapted from Carson, 1987, pp. 12–13.

women's colleges have said that one reason why women donors may not give as much to other institutions as they do to women's colleges is that the other institutions do not ask women to donate.

Consumer and demographic research

Two characteristics have been shown to have powerful effects on both consumer spending and charitable giving. People in the prime giving ages of thirty-five to sixty-four give more and spend more than other individuals, and the more income they have, the stronger is this effect. Although other factors lead specific persons to contribute to nonprofits, in the aggregate, the variables of age and income exert the strongest influence. This is why it is a good

Figure 1.5. Percentage of Women Who Donated by Race and Income Level

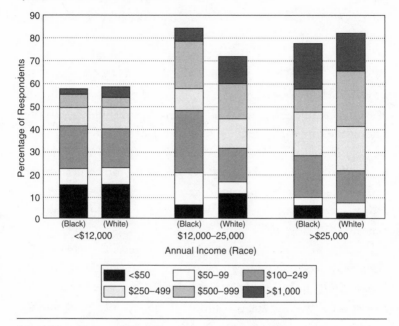

Adapted from Carson, 1987, p. 12.

idea to control for income when examining giving differences between men and women. When women earn less than men, an apparent correlation between sex and giving might actually be a correlation between income and giving. For a similar reason, a sound study about the relationship between sex and giving should also pay attention to the effect of age and control for age among the men and women in the study.

There is currently a swell in the concentration of the population that falls within the prime giving age range, and this age group is expected to experience a greater increase in income over the next decade than any other age group. Moreover, it is estimated that personal wealth in the United States in 1989 exceeded $5 trillion

(Johnson and Schwartz, 1993, p. 111). Among top wealth holders, persons aged fifty and older hold more than two-thirds of the country's total net worth. Persons sixty-five and older had a net worth of $1.6 trillion. Those in the prime giving age ranges, some of whom are already wealthy, are poised to inherit even more.

Further, though women represent fewer of the country's top wealth holders (women make up 52 percent of the total U.S. population but only 42 percent of the top wealth holders), women among the top wealth holders have fewer debts and, thus, higher average net worths than their male counterparts. Also, in 1986, women had represented only 40 percent of the top wealth holders, so there is some evidence that women are gradually gaining ground with respect to the amount of wealth they control (Johnson and Schwartz, 1993, p. 105).

In addition, more women than men now receive bachelor's and master's degrees, and education is highly correlated with income (Nasar, 1992, p. 10). In the coming decade, more married women are expected to enter the work force (Linden, 1991, p. 5), and the average earnings of working women are expected to increase (Nasar, 1992, p. 10). In 1965, women earned only sixty-five cents for every dollar men earned. By 1990, they earned sixty-nine cents per dollar. This income gap is largely attributable to the fact that these figures were generated by combining the incomes of several generations of workers. Among highly educated professionals, women earn between 95 and 99 percent as much as their male counterparts (Nasar, 1992, p. 1).

Thus, consumer and demographic data indicate that women are in an increasingly good position to be major contributors to nonprofits, but of course, the data do not say what would motivate the average woman to donate her money. The for-profit world knows more about marketing to women than does the nonprofit world. Manufacturers know that research about what motivates women to spend pays off in a major way (see Chapter Two), but there is a dearth of clear, empirical data about why women contribute to charity.

Women and foundations

Women affect giving not only via their personal gifts but also by their influence on the agendas of foundations and alternative funds and their professional work as development officers (see Chapter Three). The proportion of women on the boards or in the program offices of foundations has not changed significantly since the mid 1980s. In 1992, 29 percent of the people on program boards were women, not much more than in 1988 and only sightly more than the 24 percent representation they had a decade ago (Council on Foundations, 1992, p. 33). Women have more chances to influence foundation giving as program officers than as board members. Women nearly tripled their representation among foundation program officers during early 1980s. By 1986, they represented 60 percent of program officers, a proportion that has remained constant (Council on Foundations, 1992, p. 101).

Alternative funds may be seeing a greater increase in giving by women than are the more traditional foundations. For example, the North Star Fund, which describes itself as an alternative to "traditional foundations," and whose motto is "Change, not charity," describes its typical donor this way: "a woman with a professional career in her 30's or 40's who received income from a family business, an inheritance, a legal settlement or some unexpected source . . . also . . . older, 'mom' donors coming with their daughters and even grandparents introducing nieces and nephews to giving" (Teltsch, 1992, pp. B1, B4). The Haymarket People's Fund, a similar fund in Boston, reports that giving by women to the fund has increased 22 percent over the last three years while giving by men has remained constant. Today, women outnumber men as donors to the fund by 3.5 to 1 (Teltsch, 1992, p. B4).

Women's funds

There has also been an impressive growth in the number of women's funds, by which we mean those that promote gender equity and devote at least 75 percent of their grants to women's and girls' programs. Additionally, a women's fund has a majority of women on its board of directors, or if housed in a larger foundation, on its allocation committee. In 1985, fourteen such funds reported to the National Network of Women's Funds. By 1991, that number had increased to sixty-two (National Network of Women's Funds, 1991, p. 1).

Foundation giving

No matter how much influence women have upon foundation agendas, foundations contribute only five cents of every charitable dollar. Moreover, with the exception of the alternative funds mentioned above, men contribute to foundations more than do women. Thus, women program officers at foundations could be viewed as women spending men's money.

Needed research

The role women play as donors is just beginning to be understood. No one can yet objectively validate whether women will behave differently from men once they have full control of comparable amounts of money. However, the fact that today's development professionals are interested in the giving patterns of women is significant. Professionals often know about trends before those trends can be documented statistically. If there is a surge of interest among professional fundraisers in the giving patterns of women, that in itself indicates that there is something worth examining in women's giving.

Further, past studies of giving by women still have value even though mainly drawn from interviews. The craving for quantitative analysis may in itself be biased. Experience and anecdotal evidence are not without value. Nonetheless, the value of this kind of material can be augmented when reliable data are available. Unfortunately, current data are very limited. The giving habits of wealthy women are known through only two primary sources: case histories, interviews, and other narrative information on the one hand and quantitative data from estate records on the other. But the latter data, as we have shown here, tell more about the effects of longevity and marriage upon giving than the effects of sex on giving.

Virtually all the research available on the giving of average U.S. women comes from the Independent Sector/Gallup surveys on giving and volunteering. These studies are not designed to shed light on wealthy donors or households with incomes over $200,000. Moreover, they examine household giving patterns, and the responses of women participants are supposed to reflect household, not personal, giving. Thus, these excellent studies have been misused when they have been regarded as sources of extensive data on women's giving.

The way to find out about women as donors is not to cull from broad studies the small pieces that relate to women. The notion that these pieces tell a coherent story about women donors is wishful thinking, and the relationships the pieces may seem to show between sex and giving can be spurious and lead fundraisers astray. Instead, development professionals and others should pursue research specifically designed to study the giving behavior of women.

References

Carson, E. D. "The Contemporary Charitable Giving and Voluntarism of Black Women." Paper presented at the City University of New York Center for the Study of Philanthropy conference "Women and Philanthropy: Past, Present and Future," New York, June 17–18, 1987.

Council for Aid to Education. *Voluntary Support of Education, 1990.* New York: Council for Aid to Education, 1991.

Council for Aid to Education. *Voluntary Support of Education, 1991.* New York: Council for Aid to Education, 1992.

Council on Foundations. *The 7th Edition of the Foundation Management Report.* Washington, D.C.: Council on Foundations, 1992.

Hodgkinson, V. A., Weitzman, M. S., Noga, S. M., and Gorksi, H. A. *Giving and Volunteering in the United States: Findings from a National Survey.* Washington, D.C.: Independent Sector, 1992.

Johnson, B. W., and Rosenfeld, J. P. "Factors Affecting Charitable Giving: Inferences from Estate Tax Returns, 1986." *Trusts and Estates,* Aug. 1991, pp. 29–37.

Johnson, B. W., and Schwartz, M. "Personal Wealth, 1989." *SOI Bulletin,* Spring 1993, pp. 105–123.

Linden, F. *The Great Income Reshuffle.* New York: Conference Board, 1991.

McMillen, L. "Foundations and Corporations Concentrate Giving at Top Universities, Study Finds." *Chronicle of Higher Education,* June 5, 1991, pp. 1, 21, 23.

Nasar, S. "Women's Progress Stalled? Just Not So." *The New York Times,* Oct. 18, 1992, Section 3, pp. 1, 10.

National Network of Women's Funds. *Survey Report of Women's Funds Based on Data from 1991.* St. Paul, Minn.: National Network of Women's Funds, 1991.

Teltsch, K. "Shaking Up Old Ways of Benevolence." *New York Times,* Sept. 15, 1992, pp. B1, B4.

ANN E. KAPLAN *is the research director for the American Association of Fund-Raising Counsel (AAFRC) and the AAFRC Trust for Philanthropy and the editor of Giving USA Update.*

M. JOANNE HAYES *was president of the American Association of Fund-Raising Counsel and the AAFRC Trust for Philanthropy from 1989 to 1993.*

The new ways advertisers communicate with women and how these new ideas can be translated into development practices are examined along with gender-based personal communications. Suggestions for practical applications are offered.

2

Communicating with women: Understanding and applying the differences

Sondra C. Shaw

MADDIE GLAZER, philanthropist and national chair of the fundraising campaign for Drake University in Des Moines, Iowa, says, "Since women have become empowered, especially in the last decade, and taken their place in the leadership of our institutions and organizations, the groups they serve have changed the way they view and interact with women. Old fundraising methods are no longer successful with women who want to be involved, informed, and remain connected to a project. Communicating with women today means understanding how women see themselves, taking them seriously and talking to women in a language with which they are comfortable" (Maddie Glazer, personal interview with the author, 1992).

Development work involves communication. Whether it is with images, words, or actions, fundraisers communicate a message to their donors and prospects. Traditionally, that message has been

NEW DIRECTIONS FOR PHILANTHROPIC FUNDRAISING, NO. 2, WINTER 1993 © JOSSEY-BASS PUBLISHERS

created by men, for men. However, with women controlling a large percentage of the nation's wealth and increasing numbers of women moving into management positions, starting businesses, and earning advanced degrees, an increased awareness of female donor potential has emerged. With this awareness come fresh ways to communicate with this previously unattended donor prospect pool.

How corporations communicate with women

Women's clothing companies, like women's colleges, have long understood that women are their primary consumers. But other companies, such as athletic shoe and automobile manufacturers, have just begun to be aware of women's potential as major buyers. A similar awareness is also new to most coeducational institutions and other nonprofit organizations, which are only now beginning to realize the potential of women as major givers.

E. Janice Leeming, publisher and managing editor of the monthly newsletter *Marketing to Women*, says, "Women have more power, financially and otherwise, and advertisers are recognizing this. Our research shows women influence almost everything that is purchased" (E. Janice Leeming, telephone interview with the author, January 1993). Thus, advertising has good reason for being bent on bonding with women—women account for some 80 percent of all consumer spending in this country (Sharkey, 1993, p. 93). The messages companies in the for-profit world are communicating may be useful to fundraisers in dealing with women prospects in the nonprofit world. Following are some of the themes and gender differences these companies have identified through their research, factors that can help development officers to organize campaigns, make calls, prepare publications, and acknowledge donors.

Knowing the market

Advertisers are finding that today's women do not fit easily into a single category. According to Helayne Spivak, executive vice president and executive creative director of the Young & Rubicam advertising agency, "There is no way of saying to women today: This is you. As a result, advertisers are scrambling to keep up with women and capture and reflect the changes they're going through and their diversity as consumers" (Pomice, 1993, p. 104).

Women's magazines are using images based on demographic and psychographic profiles of their readers. Some, like *Lear's*, see their readers as educated, intelligent, and affluent. According to editor-in-chief Frances Lear, *Lear's* has "great hopes for what [the reader] can do for herself and for her community" (Lear, 1992, p. 13). Women's magazines know that during the next decade there will be a huge increase of aging baby-boomer women, and magazines like *Mirabella* and *Lear's* are preparing to meet that challenge (Krafft, 1991).

Using a different approach

Julie Newton-Cucchi, creative director for the Ogilvy & Mather advertising agency, says that "some corporations are changing the way they approach women because women are becoming new and strong consumers for big ticket items. They now buy more than just soap and toothpaste" (Julie Newton-Cucchi, telephone interview with the author, January 1993). In 1989, Nike used superstar female athletes to attract more women's business—an approach that had worked successfully with male buyers, who rushed to buy shoes endorsed by superstar male basketball players. Kate Bednarski, manager for Nike's women's division, says, "we tried to mimic what we had done with men," and she admits the campaign that attempted to make a hero out of triathlete Joanne Ernst "was a flop." Customers said, "You make great men's stuff, but I don't feel you understand me" (Zinn, 1991, p. 90).

This initial failure led to the popular $12 million print campaign created to show that Nike *did* understand women. This winning campaign stressed building self-esteem through exercise and urged women to accept themselves as they are rather than trying to achieve physical perfection. The campaign also focused on "building a relationship" with women, according to an industry journal (Caniglia, 1993, p. 1). The ads have been also described as "sitting down for a quick, refreshing booster chat with yourself, your best friend and your therapist all in one" (Caniglia, 1993, p. 1). This approach has been a major success. Nike's sales to women jumped 25 percent in 1990, the first full year of the campaign. They grew by another 25 percent in 1991 and by 28 percent in 1992, making sales to women one of the company's fastest-growing segments (Pomice, 1993, p. 103).

Communicating women's values

Some corporations have begun communicating differently with women based on what they perceive as female values and attitudes. The upscale designer Donna Karan, for example, crafted a campaign in 1992 that portrayed a young woman running for and winning the U.S. presidency. Karan explained that the next segment of the ad campaign would show the woman doing her job as president. "Maybe she'll be working with children," said Karan. "Maybe with the homeless. Maybe she'll be dealing with the environment. Whatever it is, she's got to be actually doing something, making a real difference" (Clarke, 1992, p. 15).

Toyota has been effectively reaching out to women through its ads. The company uses themes of nurturing, women and girls, developing relationships, and diversity. One ad for the campaign entitled "I Love What You Do for Me" focuses on relationships by showing a woman standing with other women beside a Toyota. The headline reads, "This Could Be the Start of a Beautiful Relationship." An ad appearing in *The Wall Street Journal* for the campaign "Investing in the Individual" presented a young black woman who received a scholarship from Toyota through the United Negro College Fund. Toyota can boast that women now purchase over 60 percent of the company's cars.

Safety is another feature Toyota and other car companies are stressing in their appeal to women. When Laurel Cutler became vice president of consumer affairs at Chrysler in the 1980s, she successfully lobbied to put air bags into cars, a move that helped bolster sagging sales. "[The need for air bags] would have been perfectly clear to any woman," she says. Volvo, with its heavy stress on safety, also appeals strongly to women (Pomice, 1993, p. 107).

E. Janice Leeming predicts that the values of the nineties will be "women's values," which she defines as accountability for decision making, responsibility, saving the environment, and family values. She believes advertisers will have to speak to those values through not only their advertising but also their corporate conduct, and says, "Corporations are even now beginning to understand that women will pay more for a product that is manufactured by a socially responsible company" (E. Janice Leeming, telephone interview with the author, January 1993).

Communicating women's images

The images of women that advertisers use have traditionally reflected the life-styles and values of the times. These images have ranged from fairly independent women in the 1920s (during the flapper age and before the Great Depression of the 1930s) and 1940s (when women took men's jobs during World War II) to the dependent homemaker-wife-mother images of the 1950s and the "superwoman" of the 1980s. Not all of the advertisers' images have accurately matched women's self-perceptions. Many have reflected what men thought women were thinking or images men themselves wanted to see. For example, in the 1960s, while women were demonstrating and reading Betty Friedan's *The Feminine Mystique*, they were portrayed in ads as being saved by the Man from Glad and wanting to look good so they could land a husband. By using images that accurately portray the many roles and responsibilities of women today, corporate America is beginning to acknowledge the importance of knowing how women see themselves. According to sociologist Jill Grigsby, "businesses that target women need to understand how women see themselves. Advertisers must present images of the American woman that acknowledge her many responsibilities without belittling any of them" (Grigsby, 1992, p. 8).

Women communicating with women

Do women communicate better with and to each other? Levi's took a woman-to-woman approach in an ad campaign that debuted in 1991. Levi's had found that women did not know the company made jeans for women, and it commissioned eight women artists for the campaign. According to Peter Angelos, creative director for the ad agency Foote, Cone & Belding, the agency chose women artists because, "as men, we like to think we're sensitive about women's issues, but we wanted the extra thought and extra sensitivity that women would have" (Helbig, 1992, p. G5).

As part of the overall strategy of reintroducing jeans to women, Levi's spokesperson Jill Novak Lynch said, "the campaign had to be respectful to women, and Levi's believed the best people to speak to a group are people who belong to that group." The line drawings in blue, black, and white show women doing everyday things like reading the newspaper, because Levi's "asked artists to portray women doing things the average viewer would have experienced. It's easier to place yourself in the ad if it's something you have done." And Lynch adds that "there has been a definite increase in sales."

Appreciation for special roles

Corporations like Dean Witter are using advertising in women's magazines to acknowledge the contribution of women to their communities and their professions. For example, Dean Witter credits women's long-standing roles as volunteers and professionals through an ad that says, "We're Looking for Dedicated People, Like Rene Nourse." The ad goes on to explain that Nourse has a tremendous sense of community responsibility, demonstrated through her dedication to a local social services organization for which she works as a board member and financial officer.

Sara Lee Corporation annually takes out a full-page ad in *The New York Times* to showcase its Frontrunner awards, given to women who best embody the "qualities of strength, balance and integrity." The ad reads: "We admire their accomplishments. We share their spirit. We celebrate their lives." Through these awards, Sara Lee recognizes the value of women's emotional strength and integrity and their capacity to balance work and family. Sara Lee carries out this recognition with not only an advertising campaign but also a ceremony, a celebration.

Sprint/United Telecom publicizes its outstanding record as an equal opportunity employer through a campaign entitled "It's a New World." An ad in this campaign, printed in an executive women's magazine, says, "After looking into our hiring practices, leading civil rights groups decided to make an example of us." The ad goes on to say that these groups include leading women's groups. As part of the campaign, Sprint/United Telecom talks about the rich diversity its employees bring to the company.

Women's clothing manufacturer Esprit not only uses ads that deal with social issues, but owner Susie Tompkins also gives her employees ten hours off a month to do volunteer work and has a new collection of clothes called Ecollection, made as environmentally sound as possible. Tompkins says, "as a businesswoman [I am] trying to use my company as a vehicle to inspire good values and social change. I would love to be a role model. I hope that other companies will see what we're doing and learn from us" (Lear, 1992, p. 13)

Communicating by asking questions

When newspapers found that over the last ten years fewer women were reading their pages, they too began to be more sensitive to women's influence. They turned to focus groups to find out what they could do to halt the decline in readership, and what they discovered, says Marjorie David, editor of the Sunday *Chicago Tribune*'s *Womanews* magazine, was that women, "didn't feel reflected" in the newspaper (personal communication, January 1993). Information from the focus groups led to *Womanews*, which has an all-woman staff committed to reflecting its readers through images and topics.

Applying corporate experience to nonprofit fundraising

Many in the corporate world are recognizing that marketing and advertising to women requires a change from "business as usual." The nonprofit world can learn from this experience. In the same way as corporations gained sales by regarding women as important consumers, development professionals have much to gain by looking at women as potentially important prospects and finding new ways to approach and communicate with them.

Knowing the market

Targeting for diversity is worthwhile for fundraisers. As newspapers have found in their efforts to win back women readers, it is difficult to target women as a single group (Pearl, 1992, p. B1). One way fundraisers can target women is by breaking the female population into age groups and developing programs for each one. The younger career women and homemakers might have a lunch group whose purposes range from mentoring girls and becoming comfortable with financial matters to fundraising. The middle-aged group's program would take fundraising more seriously, provide leadership training to other women, and become sophisticated about the financial advantages of philanthropy. An older women's group might fundraise and learn the thrill of giving and, through this activity, become empowered.

What is the best approach?

Development officers can take their lead from the ways magazines approach their women readers. Susan Krafft, associate editor of *American Demographics*, says that the ways magazines communicate with women include speaking to them as being thoughtful and sensible, having a caring nature, or looking for solutions and strategies for living (Krafft, 1991, p. 47). As development officers communicate their programs and strategies, it is important that they keep these factors in mind and be prepared to discuss reasons why a program is crucial, why it is or is not a collaborative effort, whom it may help, and how it might make the world a better place.

As development officers approach older women donors in particular, it may be necessary for them to consider the context of the women's life experiences and use a realistic message that empowers these women as philanthropists. Development officers need prospects and donors (both women and men) who are capable of making their own well thought-out decisions about programs that need support. Just as advertisers are mindful of using respect when directing their messages to women, so too should fundraisers communicate respect for and honesty about donors' needs and experiences.

Incorporating women's values in development programs

Recent anecdotal research about women's values as they relate to philanthropy reveal that women give from the heart: they want to make a difference, and they want the world to be a better place in which to bring up children (Shaw and Taylor, 1991; Stone and Sublett, 1993). These are the same themes that appear in advertisers' views of what women value, through, for example, photos of children, women, and girls that show diversity and concern for the environment.

The advertisers' experience also suggests that development officers must continually reassess their programs and messages to be sure they are addressing those things women consider important. Do the programs offer women choices in areas that will interest them and make a difference? If so, are development officers adequately conveying their message about these values through their publications and in their telephone calls? Just as Sprint/United Telecom communicates with women about the company's encouragement of diversity, professional development officers should be aware of programs within their organizations and institutions that promote multiculturalism and help address social problems. By publicizing these programs, development officers give women an opportunity to participate and support the program efforts.

Communicating an institution's image

Review of publications' articles and pictures to make sure they regularly include a representation of women and diversity will demonstrate an institution's commitment to a world in which women also have power and presence. When fundraisers recognize women in publications, they also provide an opportunity for these women to be represented as role models.

A more complex but substantive approach is an ongoing examination of the number of women on institutions' boards and in their administrations; of the ways women fit into long-range plans, programs, and fundraising efforts; of organizational commitment to engaging and involving women; and of the amount of resources dedicated to all these issues. Only when an institution takes seriously the effort to involve more women on boards and staff will that institution's image be perceived to show commitment to helping and including women.

Just as advertisers are seeing the necessity of presenting images of U.S. women that accurately portray these women's many roles and responsibilities, fundraising organizations must be sure they are realistically representing women in both institutional publications and decision-making groups.

Communicating appreciation for women's special roles

Women tend to volunteer before they give, and fundraising efforts should recognize this important aspect of what women consider meaningful to their lives. Acknowledging women's voluntary contributions as well as their financial ones validates the importance of these volunteer efforts. Fundraisers could also give awards to women who volunteer, contribute, and successfully balance a life of family, work, community service, and philanthropy. What better way to show an appreciation of women's multifaceted role in today's society and to express gratitude for the connections women have forged with a particular charitable organization?

Advantages of women communicating with women

When fundraisers communicate one-on-one with women donors, an important communication tool is the ability to ask questions. According to Marjorie David of *Womanews*, "there is a difference in the kinds of questions men and women ask in covering stories. A man

doesn't think of asking women what they think" (personal communication, 1993). Women, however, "touch on relationships. They
want to gain facts too, but they also want to know how people feel
about what is happening." To demonstrate interest in women
prospects and gain valuable information about fundraising organizations, fundraisers should look for opportunities to ask such open-
ended questions as, How do you see this organization? How do you
see yourself relating to this project? Do you have any questions you
would like to ask me? Is there anything further I can provide for you?

Participating and sharing their ideas in focus groups seem to
have particular appeal for women, and such groups are also being
used in the new model capital campaign. For example, Thomas G.
Fox, vice president for development and public affairs at Oregon
Health Sciences University, developed a "focused affinity strategy,"
using the empowerment concepts from W. Edwards Deming's
fourteen points of Total Quality Management. In Fox's program,
focus groups defined need, developed strategy, and produced a
common communication between staff and volunteers (Fox, 1992).
In contrast to the structured and hierarchical capital campaigns of
the past, this technique allowed more involvement of and participation by women.

Use of such techniques builds volunteer participation and empowerment and gives volunteer fundraisers confidence in building
a case for support, making the call, and asking for funds. In turn,
such volunteer confidence can propel a development program to
the cutting edge of fundraising. Equally important are strategies to
bring women into campaigns with methods the women understand
and with which they feel comfortable.

New ways of communicating

There are a number of similarities between the nonprofit world
and the advertising industry. Both are ever in need of more
clients/customers and prospects/donors. Both are always looking
for convincing ways to tell their stories. Changes in life-styles and

people's values strongly impact the work of both. And both are always striving to catch up with what is going on in the world so they can better define and communicate their messages.

Messages used to successfully engage customers may help development officers communicate better with their women donors and prospects. Development officers can learn from the business world that some approaches work better for women, and so these officers, too, should respond to women's special interests and needs. When fundraisers strive to empower women as philanthropists, they also give women an opportunity to make the world a better place.

References

Caniglia, J. "Buy, Buy, Miss American Pie." *Isthmus*, Feb. 19, 1992, p. 1.

Clarke, C. "Karan's Commander-in-Chic." *Working Woman*, June 1992, p. 15.

Fox, T. "Focused Affinity Strategy: An Alternative to the Capital Campaign." *CASE Currents*, Oct. 1992, p. 54.

Grigsby, J. "Women Change Places." *American Demographics*, Nov. 1992, p. 8.

Helbig, B. "Levi's Takes a Woman to Woman Approach." *Wisconsin State Journal*, Oct. 27, 1992, p. G5.

Krafft, S. "Window on a Woman's Mind." *American Demographics*, Dec. 1991, p. 47.

Lear, F. "Lunch." *Lear's*, July 1992, p. 13.

Nichols, J. *Changing Demographics: Fund Raising in the 1990's*. Chicago: Bonus Books, 1990.

Pearl, D. "Newspapers Strive to Win Back Women." *The Wall Street Journal*, May 4, 1992, p. B1.

Pomice, E. "A Few Good Women: And How They're Changing the Way Advertising Addresses Us." *Lear's*, Mar. 1993, pp. 103–107.

Sharkey, B. "You've Come a Long Way, Madison Avenue." *Lear's*, Mar. 1993, pp. 93–101.

Shaw, S., and Taylor, M. "Career Women: A Changing Environment for Philanthropy." *NSFRE Journal*, Fall 1991, pp. 43–49.

Stone, K., and Sublett, D. "The UCLA Women and Philanthropy Focus Groups Report." Unpublished report. Office of Development, University of California, Los Angeles, 1993.

Zinn, L. "This Bud's for You. No, Not You—Her." *Business Week*, Nov. 4, 1991, pp. 86, 90.

SONDRA C. SHAW *is an attorney, cofounder of the National Network of Women as Philanthropists, and director of development and state relations at the State Historical Society of Wisconsin.*

*The increased number of women in chief develop-
ment officer positions has had a positive effect on the
fundraising field. The skills and personal attributes
necessary for success are examined, with an emphasis on the characteristics that make women particularly well suited to the profession.*

3

Women as staff leaders and fundraisers

Paula J. Faust, H. Sargent Whittier, Jr.

WHILE MOST CHAPTERS in this volume address the role of women
as volunteers and donors, women also often bring uniquely female
approaches to fundraising staff leadership, and as professional staff
members of nonprofit organizations, women have made a significant impact on philanthropy. Although their individual skills, personality, experience, intellectual power, character, and other attributes have influenced their success, the best of the women in
leading staff roles complement their personal individual traits with
valuable characteristics that are generally thought to be more female than male.

This chapter is based on the collective and anecdotal experiences
of nine women who hold top development positions in a variety of
nonprofit organizations across the United States (Appendix A, at
the end of this chapter, lists these women and their positions). Each
woman was selected because of her broad understanding of the

NEW DIRECTIONS FOR PHILANTHROPIC FUNDRAISING, NO. 2, WINTER 1993 © JOSSEY-BASS PUBLISHERS

field, practical and direct experience, and recognized success. In telephone interviews, the nine women responded to a set of questions about their own careers and made observations about the topic in general (Appendix B, at the end of this chapter, lists the questions asked). The conversations began with general questions about the skills and personal qualities necessary for success in the field of development and moved to both more specific and more subjective questions about gender differences. We also asked these handpicked women to make judgments about the reasons for their own success.

Although our findings are not in the least scientific, fundraisers who are considering the complex issue of women and philanthropy will nevertheless find the women's observations important. Our discussions went beyond the questions to such topics as compensation, where women can go after success in development (happily, women are also achieving success as leaders of nonprofit organizations, private foundations, and educational institutions), and the balance between professional and personal life.

"Plainly the nonprofit sector, as well as government, offers proportionately more opportunities for employment for women and minorities [than the for-profit sector]," observes Mirvis (1992, p. 39), and the introduction of women on the development staffs of colleges and universities in significant numbers in the mid to late 1970s began a trend that has continued. At the same time, women's presence is adding a new texture to fundraising, both within the organizations women serve and in the field as women work with board members, other volunteers, and supporters. In the summer of 1973, four of the 100 participants at a meeting sponsored by the American Alumni Council for newcomers to development were women. By "1988, women outnumbered men in the field" (Hall, 1992, p. 1).

Women are increasingly being tapped for top development positions and performing in them successfully. Most women in leadership positions today have held a variety of positions and come up through the ranks. While this career progression took time, the women we interviewed say that this career path means that women in development have brought with them an in-depth understanding of fundamentals.

Unsung heroes

In its infancy in the late 1950s and early 1960s, the development business attracted staff, predominantly male, from other roles and careers. In many instances, learning by hit or miss, the wives of these development officers and of nonprofit institutions' presidents performed many of the tasks now considered essential to fundraising success. In the early years of advancement of the development profession, there were many involved, hard-working, uncompensated women who "worked the crowd"; remembered names, connections, and affiliations; and often influenced the timing and purpose of solicitations. Female support staff, too, provided important background on potential donors and worked behind the scenes to help advance the cause. Clearly, these unsung heroes demonstrated the kinds of social skills, motivations, and sensitivity that would enhance the effectiveness of the increasing number of women entering the professional development ranks. Among the women we interviewed, some moved into development positions from each of the roles mentioned here. They had both observed the development process and participated in development. They also brought with them the social skills acquired in their support positions. Highly motivated and curious, they learned the skills necessary to advance in their own careers while advancing the missions of the institutions that employed them. They say they had an appreciation of the many facets of the work and a willingness to give credit to others.

Some men in positions of responsibility for hiring staff became open to women as candidates. At the same time, development staffs were growing, so there was a need to hire and train new talent. Still, some men who wanted to and ultimately did hire women did so at risk to their own standing in the organization. Stories about men who gave women a break and who opened closed doors are numerous among our interviewees. Women began to be recruited out of college for development positions. The workplace culture was also changing rapidly, to the surprise of many traditionalists. One woman remembered her first fundraising trip: her male boss told her to "make friends," but she figured that what she needed was information. On her early trip reports he wrote, "These are extraordinary." Her thoughtful businesslike approach seemed to surprise him. For other women, it was their male bosses who became mentors, showed them the ropes, and helped them succeed at every step. Donors and potential donors, mostly men who had few, if any, female colleagues, usually accepted women development officers and responded positively to their thoughtful, forthright, open, and reasoned requests for involvement as volunteers and donors.

Building relationships

The business of development is building real and lasting relationships. Consequently, it is generally acknowledged that communication skills are key to success. In *The Female Advantage*, Sally Helgesen writes that "workplaces run by women tend to be webs of inclusion. Male leaders tend to champion the value of vision, women leaders concentrate on developing a voice" (1990, p. 47). There are growing numbers of studies and writings about women and men in the workplace and their differences in style and approach, and some studies that cite the different ways in which women and men communicate have become popular sellers today (for example, Deborah Tannen's book *You Just Don't Understand*). In her interview, Susan L. Washburn, former chair of the Council for Advancement and Support of Education (CASE), pointed out the female trait that she feels is central to the unusual success women have enjoyed in the development field: "Women establish connections on an emotional or personal level more quickly than do men. Therefore, they are more likely to discuss and learn about primary interests and real motivations. Prospects generally do not share the same things with a man, at least initially, as they feel permission to share with a woman."

Important skills and personal attributes

Seven of the nine women we interviewed put "people skills" at the top of their lists of traits for successful development officers. People skills may be difficult to define, but the ability to relate well with people on a variety of levels requires at least curiosity, empathy, interest, sincerity, and the ability to communicate. It is no surprise that the ability to communicate was mentioned by most respondents, and listening skills were singled out as more important than speaking or writing skills. Particularly experienced and successful development officers learned early in their careers the essential value of listening, and what fundraisers are now learning suggests that women often come to the field with this ability more fully developed than it is among men. Our respondents also referred to other skills required, including organizational skills, which appeared on several lists; like people skills, organizational skills are hard to define but nevertheless essential. They refer to the ability to manage a variety of other people and projects and a volume of detail simultaneously.

Knowledge of financial matters, computers, planned giving, and the laws governing philanthropy was mentioned as important. A solid grounding in fundraising techniques and the literature of philanthropy was considered essential. Given the right opportunities, an understanding of the fundamentals of development can be readily acquired. Coming to grips with the human and personal attributes required of a development officer and exercising these attributes effectively is a more difficult dimension of acquiring development skills. This difficulty is precisely why successful people in the field, including all of the women interviewed, talk about the need for intellectual curiosity, openness, and flexibility as well as the need for a set of personal values that fit well with the fundraising institution's values. Such qualities help shape a person's character, and it is a good personal character that builds credibility and confidence with volunteers, potential donors, and colleagues. It allows fundraisers to develop the real rapport and lasting relationships that help to motivate donors to act philanthropically.

Fundraising is, and should be, more art than science. While there is a growing body of knowledge about the field and an increasingly important collection of technical tools, proficiency with such tools is not necessarily a formula for success. Understanding the differences between people and listening and caring about individual motivations and personal goals is the personal ability that makes the difference. Learning how potential donors, volunteers, and colleagues make and execute—or fail to make—decisions is critical to success. Common sense is critical, and "the thing you have to remember about common sense is that it is so uncommon" (Whitesell, 1992, p. 8).

Characteristics that make women well suited for development

Are there any characteristics that help women to be particularly successful in development positions? Most of the women with whom we talked responded yes unhesitatingly. Two said no. Then, upon reflection, some interviewees qualified their answers. For some who believe success depends more on personality than on gender, such a question provokes ambivalence because individuals succeed for individual reasons. Still, seven of the nine respondents had no trouble saying with conviction that, in their experience, women are particularly well suited for development. Many believe women have better people skills. As Nancy White McCabe said, "women are willing to rank the good of the group at least as high as good of the self. Women have a special ability to tolerate ambiguity."

Some respondents also believed that women are capable of performing multiple tasks successfully, a quality that is important because leadership positions in development require such facility. Several of the interviewees said women have a tendency to work especially hard. One mentioned a bias toward hiring women because they will take on the tough jobs and carry them through to completion. Some think "detail" and "big picture" skills are more likely to coexist in women than in men.

"Adaptability" and "nurturing" were words many interviewees used. Because women tend to think of the needs of others, they make donors feel that the development officer is more interested in them than in the bottom line. "We are by socialization, not genetics, dependent upon relationship building," said Karen E. Osborne. That same socialization, Susan L. Washburn remarked, "makes women nurturing, sensitive beings in tune with the complexities of both verbal and nonverbal messages." In addition, whether it is a female attribute or simply an understanding of the development business, women seem to accept the role of being in the background more easily than men do. A successful development officer is a person who orchestrates, often from behind the scenes, actions that move people along a continuum from interest to involvement to support.

It may be that women have intuition that is not readily found in men. Because of the ways in which women are raised, the culture they inherit, and societal expectations, women's view of life and living may, in fact, be different from their male counterparts' view. Some who write about the managerial differences between men and women cite the differences in the games boy and girl children play or the way they are treated in school as influences. Perhaps the characteristics that seem more common to women than men are biological. We believe that it is probably a combination of biology, culture, and each individual's unique personality traits and sets of experience that contributes to individual women's success.

Gender and becoming a development officer

The debate about gender-linked differences will continue among cultural anthropologists, psychologists, biologists, historians, and other social scientists, but there are other gender-linked issues that our respondents believe they have noted. In particular, there is the issue of how the respondents reached their present positions.

Helgesen writes that "women describe themselves as trusting that the opportunities that come their way will unlock their futures. Like the ancient female goddesses, they understand that the future cannot be reduced to a simple matter of objectives, nor achieved by the mere application of will" (1990, p. 60). Yet Colette M. Murray, who has been in fundraising for twenty-three years (longer than any of the other women interviewed), said, "in all honesty, gender has not played a role in my success." Also a former chair of CASE, she had been a volunteer and was an attorney when she entered the development field. "I may have gotten interviewed because I was a woman," she said, "but I always got the job because of my skills."

However, Murray believes that women have succeeded particularly well perhaps because there were higher standards for women in the beginning. She felt that "women still have to prove themselves as managers," and other respondents voiced similar beliefs. For example, Murray pointed out that "people of both sexes, in checking references on potential job candidates, probe this area by asking different questions about women than they do about men." Some of the interviewees were promoted not because of gender but in spite of it.

Most of the group with whom we spoke began their careers in fundraising between 1974 and 1977. Only one started later, in 1981. Four moved into development from positions in university administration, three started in traditionally female occupations (mother, special education teacher, and lab technician), and one came to development from a bank management training program.

Four of the nine women have held more than one chief development position since they entered the field.

More of the respondents believe that gender has influenced their effectiveness as a fundraiser than believe that it has played a role in their career success. Of course, the two achievements are very closely related. In this field, one-on-one success with donors and volunteers has everything to do with career success. Respondents' observations about their effectiveness as one-on-one fundraisers range from Sally Souris's remark that "it is at the close [of asking for a gift] where gender really makes a difference; prospects are amazed a woman would ask the tough question" to this comment from Karen Osborne: "I have gotten into homes no one had gotten into before, and I could work with both spouses." The feminine attributes of candor, nurturing acceptance, and strong listening and people skills contribute to our notion that women are indeed particularly well suited to development.

Compensation inequity

Studies show that women fundraisers, in the aggregate, are less well compensated than their male counterparts. But, interestingly enough, most of our respondents said that was not true in their own cases. Clearly, then, the group we selected is not representative. Still, the response is reassuring. It appears, admittedly with limited evidence, that very competent women who compete for and succeed in important development jobs can also command requisite compensation. At the top of the development profession, and when differences in qualifications, experience, and competence are factored in, the gap in compensation seems to have narrowed.

Many of the respondents said, in effect, "we are not good negotiators for ourselves." This is ironic, given the nature of development work and the everyday role negotiation plays in dealing with board members, other volunteers, donors, and colleagues. The failure to negotiate well for oneself may be yet another example of women's tendency to put the needs of others ahead of their own. Negotiating appropriate compensation for themselves is a skill women can and should develop. One interviewee told a story about a former boss calling her in to say, "I am not happy with the job you are doing." Fighting back tears, she then heard him say, "I want to promote you." She was so grateful to have the job, she accepted a large increase in responsibility but failed to negotiate commensurately higher compensation.

It seems from conversations with the interviewees that the need for acceptance and approval is a bigger issue with women than with men. This nation's current transition from a largely male work force to an integrated work force reveals such issues and requires both individual and collective response.

Cream rises to the top

As in many other fields, it has taken a long time for women to reach top positions. For talented women, their taking the time to learn about the various aspects of the craft and to prepare more fully for broader responsibilities has served them well, even though they may not have had the goal of becoming chief development officers clearly in mind. When they reached chief development positions, they were both well schooled in the fundamentals and well prepared by personal disposition and the positive female attributes cited earlier.

Many women development officers came to their responsibilities with fresh perspectives unencumbered by membership in the old boys' networks. They traded on positive thinking and, like the best of their male counterparts, were goal oriented, optimistic, able to inspire others to act, and possessed of a generosity of spirit. These, among others, are qualities necessary for real success in development. The world of philanthropy discovered a generation of women fundraisers who stepped up to their responsibilities fully ready for the challenges.

Staff perspective

The issues surrounding women as donors that are raised in this volume are very much on the minds of the women with whom we spoke. The respondents have given careful thought to the issues, and all volunteered general observations. Ann Caldwell, the first woman chief development officer in the Ivy League, said that "when women see themselves in equal numbers as trustees and leaders, larger gifts from women will follow." Certainly, the number of women who are leaders on the staff side of development is increasing, and those women who attain those leadership positions are, through their success, paving the way for other women to follow.

Lest development officers forget the essence of development, however, Karen Osborne issues this reminder: "I've been hearing a great deal about women being different as donors. That has always struck me as false. We hurt ourselves when we segment and think we need a separate strategy for women—people are individuals! Let's not make a big mistake—there are differences, to be sure—but the individual differences should take priority."

The discussions reported here are not a controlled research study and should not be seen as such. They provide useful insights into the ways in which nine individuals who have risen to the position of chief development officer and who happen to be female view their own success and that of other women. Yet, as interesting and potentially useful as these observations are, they leave the overall issue where it began. It is difficult at best and perhaps will remain impossible to make generalizations about gender differences and their effects. Even as the scientifically designed research continues and deepens, the "truth" will remain elusive. There are too many variables. The harder development officers look for the "truth," the more they may realize that the human differences, personal chemistry, interpersonal chemistry, and the luck of time and place are *all* important. Development is more art than science. We hope that belief will remain central to future deliberations of this topic.

Women's influence

Fundraising has become a leading field in providing access and opportunity for women. Few fundraisers are surprised that bright,
competent people who have chosen development are successful.
More are surprised to discover that some of the perspectives
women bring to the field have had a profound influence on the
thinking in the field about both the qualities desirable in development officers and the manner in which the work can be approached. By recognizing these special perspectives, practitioners
have a clearer picture of the motivations of both volunteers and
donors.

Appendix A: Women development officers interviewed

Ann W. Caldwell, vice president for development, Brown University, Providence, R.I.

Rebecca Girvin-Argon, executive director, Museum Center
Foundation, Cincinnati, Ohio

Charlotte B. Heartt, director of development, Smith College,
Northampton, Mass.

Nancy White McCabe, director of development, The Guggen-
heim Foundation, New York, N.Y.

Colette M. Murray, corporate vice president for philanthropy
and communication, Henry Ford Health Systems, Detroit,
Mich.

Karen E. Osborne, vice president for institutional advancement,
Trinity College, Hartford, Conn.

Susan Pearce, vice president Music Center Unified Fund, Los Angeles Music Center, Los Angeles, Calif.

Sally V. Souris, vice chancellor for advancement, State System of Higher Education, Harrisburg, Pa.

Appendix B: Text of telephone interview introduction and questions

My call to you is prompted by my work with several others on a new Jossey-Bass book on philanthropy. I have been asked to author a chapter in the book, and the opinions of a variety of development professionals will help to make the work more realistic and meaningful. I would be grateful if you would give me about ten minutes to discuss some specific questions. Should we choose to use any of your observations and attribute them to you, be assured that we will seek your approval of the specific text.

1. How many years have you worked in fundraising?
2. For how long have you held your present position?
3. What did you do before you got into this field?
4. What do you believe are the most important skills a successful development officer should possess?
5. What do you believe are the personal attributes most critical for success?
6. Are there characteristics that make women particularly well suited for development?
7. Has gender played a role in the success of your career? If so, how?
8. Has gender influenced your effectiveness as a fundraiser? If so, how?
9. The book on which I am working will deal with the many aspects of the involvement of women in philanthropy. Specifi-

cally, this chapter will focus on the contributions women have made to the development profession and the ways in which their involvement as chief development officers has influenced the practice of fundraising. With that in mind, do you have any other observations that might be useful?

References

Hall, H. "Women's New Charity Clout." *Chronicle of Philanthropy*, June 16, 1992, p. 1.

Helgesen, S. *The Female Advantage*. New York: Doubleday, 1990.

Mirvis, P. H. "The Quality of Employment in the Nonprofit Sector: An Update on Employee Attitudes in Nonprofit Versus Business and Government." *Nonprofit Management and Leadership*, 1992, *3* (1), 23–41.

Whitesell, W. "Clinton Needs to Create More Jobs, Economics Professors Advise." *The Gazette*, Franklin and Marshall College, Dec. 1992, pp. 7–9.

PAULA J. FAUST *is director of development and public affairs at the Thomas Jefferson Memorial Foundation.*

H. SARGENT WHITTIER, JR., *is senior vice president, Barnes & Roche, Inc.*

The motivations and attitudes that influence wom-
en's philanthropic behavior are explored through
data drawn from focus group studies conducted by
the Women and Philanthropy Program at the
University of California, Los Angeles.

4

Women's approach to philanthropy: A learning model

Dyan Sublett

This is one thing women have to do. . . . Women have
to love other women. Women have to allow women to
be wherever the hell they are . . . housewife, widow,
professional . . . as long as we end up with a world we
can all live in.
—PARTICIPANT, UCLA WOMEN AND PHILANTHROPY
FOCUS GROUP

CONTEMPORARY EXAMINATIONS of women's styles of communication, leadership strategies, and developmental paths suggest that
women may have their own unique approaches to philanthropy as
well. What motivates women to make significant gifts? How do
women learn and then pass on philanthropic behavior? What are
the values women bring to their philanthropic commitments? In
order to answer these questions, as well as to involve women as
fuller participants in the life of the university, the Women and Philanthropy Program at the University of California, Los Angeles,
designed a series of focus groups in which women's philanthropic

NEW DIRECTIONS FOR PHILANTHROPIC FUNDRAISING, NO. 2, WINTER 1993 © JOSSEY-BASS PUBLISHERS

attitudes might be fully explored. Although our initial focus was on research, we quickly recognized that the learning we undertook was a powerful reciprocal process: while we gained an understanding of the elements that informed women's philanthropic decisions, the women themselves were brought to an understanding of their own potency as philanthropists. The focus groups offered an environment supportive of exploration and, implicitly, of women's values. At the same time as we created an opportunity for women to become comfortable with themselves as philanthropists, we also initiated a critical stage of cultivation for the university's most important women donors. The study documenting the focus group, "The UCLA Women and Philanthropy Focus Groups Report" (Stone and Sublett, 1992), provides further detail regarding women's particular needs and responses during the cultivation and solicitation stages.

Initiating the focus group study

Four factors contributed significantly to the success of UCLA's focus group study: a carefully prepared instrument of questions, a professional focus group facilitator, a first-class facility designed specifically for focus group work, and a follow-up session in which findings were reported back to the women participants.

First, to help us devise the interview instrument, we enlisted a team of educators and market researchers. Several months were dedicated to clarifying what we wanted to know, linking our various areas of interest, and refining the query techniques that would most effectively elicit the information we sought. This process also provided a valuable focus to our efforts, ultimately defining the approach that would become our foundation.

Second, and perhaps most important of all, we selected a professional facilitator who would assume responsibility for leading the focus groups. It was the facilitator who created an atmosphere for candid exchange, encouraging reluctant voices, probing with sensitivity, and leading the group back to key themes. While the facilitator did her work, my codirector and I, along with other development directors, were freed to sit behind the one-way glass of the conference room, invisible observers of the women's conversations.

Third, it was crucial to have a facility that was designed to accommodate our groups comfortably. It was equipped with spacious and well-appointed conference rooms, one-way glass, an observers' room, and audio recording equipment, as well as other amenities that effectively communicated the seriousness of our work. The building was located in a desirable neighborhood, adjacent to a restaurant where we could host a private cocktail reception. Although the reception was initially designed as a gesture of graciousness, we quickly learned how critical it was for the women in the focus groups to continue their conversations with one another. Information was carried through, and new friendships were forged. We would not now underestimate the role that the facility and the social time play in creating a positive experience for both study participants and directors.

We promised to share what we had learned with the participants in a report-back session at the conclusion of the focus group study, and it was this follow-up action that emerged as the fourth element of the project's success. A full seventy of the seventy-six program participants attended a hotel reception cohosted by one of UCLA's women philanthropists. The participants were offered a presentation of findings, the report document, and musical theater entertainment by students who were themselves recipients of fellowships established by a woman philanthropist. Most of all, the women had an opportunity to come together again, renewing contacts and sharing perceptions of how their participation in the study has informed their work as donors, volunteers, and trustees.

Criteria for selection of participants included philanthropic experience at a donor level of $25,000 or above, a demonstrated understanding of philanthropic goals, and a connection to UCLA as a donor, volunteer, or alumna. A total of 285 women were initially selected by development officers, deans, and other academic and administrative leaders, with 76 eventually participating. Six focus groups were conducted, representing respondents from various demographic backgrounds. As a result of the selection criteria, the economic statuses of participants tended to be similar. In addition, most women had either devoted considerable time and resources to the university or had identified themselves as emerging leaders in the UCLA community. Although there was a mix of social, cul-tural, religious, professional, and other backgrounds, the selection criteria resulted in only a modest number of young women and women of color, identifying the need for further programmatic work with women in these two particular groups.

The majority of the respondents were married or widowed, and many had children. In fact, as participants were asked to describe themselves for their group, a particular pattern of choices emerged: when applicable, women identified themselves as mothers first, noting number and gender of children, and followed that informa-tion with professional information and community- or UCLA-related activities. All respondents described themselves as heavily involved in either their profession, philanthropy, or both.

Findings from the focus group study

When women were approached by letter to participate in focus groups for UCLA's Women and Philanthropy Program, their re-sponse was unusually enthusiastic. Before the follow-up calls promised in the invitation could even begin, many invitees initi-ated their own responses, calling UCLA to make sure they would be included. The number of groups originally planned for Los An-geles was immediately doubled, and we later added Orange County, San Diego, and the San Francisco Bay Area as expanded territories. As their high level of enthusiasm indicates, the women were eager to be heard. Their stories were varied and multifaceted, reflecting their range of backgrounds, interests, and occasionally, conflicting points of view. Over time, however, particular themes emerged that identified them as a group.

Personal motive

Personal motives were most often cited as the ultimate factor in the decision to make a gift. Although all practical aspects of gift giving were examined, in intelligent and often rigorous ways, the women were ultimately influenced in their philanthropic decisions by an ethic of personal commitment. Time and again they mentioned moral belief in an organization or issue, using such words as "heart" and "passion" to convey a deeply felt response.

Tradition

Family tradition was a particularly strong theme; mothers were most often cited as giving examples. The majority of the participants indicated that giving had always been a family tradition, even if their families had only a small amount of money. Some mentioned the quarters their mothers taught them to put into the Tzedaka boxes kept in Jewish homes for various charities; others told stories about watching their mothers feed homeless men who came to their back doors during the Depression. One women said, "I grew up in a home that was middle-class, certainly not wealthy, but my mother always volunteered. . . . If you had something, it was your responsibility to give back to the community." Another said, "In my past, I have been a recipient of scholarships. I have to tell you that my mother raised six of us by herself . . . because my father died. In order to keep going, we received, and because of that I feel I have to give back. I think once you've been on the other side, if you come out of it, you come out of it with a deep sense of giving."

Teaching philanthropy

The passing on of philanthropic behavior to the next generation was a related theme consistently expressed. The women shared a concern for educating young people to what the women referred to as a responsibility for others, a giving back. Among those participants with children, a few described conscious teaching efforts, such as including adolescents in family meetings in which financial information was openly shared and philanthropic decisions made. One woman remarked, "There are really important reasons to make sure that girls in a family learn about business matters and financial matters when they're quite young. In our family, when a girl becomes sixteen, she comes to all the family investment meetings and business meetings and learns all about it. All the children do, so they know what to do." Other women commented that their children had learned by example, noting that their older offspring had already begun to give, often to environmental or political action groups. Whether or not the participants were also mothers, they were unanimous in their sense of urgency regarding the education of future generations to the responsibilities of giving. One woman commented in addition that, in her family, the children were influenced because "we get so much joy from giving to something that is meaningful to us. We get so much back—far more than we can ever give—the joy and the warmth and the gratification of giving and helping somebody, or something, and seeing that their life, or the cause, is better because of it. Our children are beginning in a very small way to do the same thing, and I think it's because they've seen how excited we get."

Personal involvement

Women will give time first, before committing to a major gift. While this is not always true when only modest gifts are given, it seems to be the way in which the participants felt most comfortable building enough trust and confidence in an organization to make a significant commitment to it. Since women are still rarely invited to enter a nonprofit's board room or join its prestigious councils, work as a volunteer is often the only vehicle available to them to test the fit between their values and interests and those of the organizations soliciting their support. One woman, in fact, went so far as to state that she had never given to any organization with which she had not been personally involved.

We observed that discussions of volunteer involvement also offered strong parallels to the historical role of women in the establishment and growth of nonprofit organizations worldwide. From Jane Addams, the founder of Hull-House, to Elizabeth Glaser, the founder of the Pediatric Aids Foundation, women have tradition- ally played the dual role of volunteer-philanthropist. Though women are now becoming more sophisticated and powerful wield- ers of the philanthropic dollar, their reasons for finding volunteer activity important remain the same as those that motivated gener- ations of women before them: to make a difference, to act respon- sibly and directly, and to have a personal impact on issues about which they care most deeply.

Wanting to make a difference

A desire to make a difference is a natural complement to the themes already discussed, and it was not surprising to find this desire re- peated over and over by the women respondents. They wanted to know the projected impact of their support and were far more in- clined to make a major gift if they were involved with the program for which they were being solicited. While they perceived men as making gifts for purposes of personal recognition or business, the women were more interested in effecting change with their giving. They wanted to provide kids in South Central Los Angeles with a college education, to bring women onto the faculty of schools of law and engineering, and to create psychological and family ser- vices for women suffering from breast cancer. One woman de- scribed her desire this way: "One of the key motivations for me is that I try to give money where I feel no one else is giving their money, and where my money will make a difference because it's not a popular thing to do, and not something that confers status, but something that I believe will make a change."

Recognition in one's own right

Gift recognition was an area that had often caused respondents to discontinue giving because of errors or omissions. One woman had "stopped giving to organizations" that insisted on thanking her husband. She said, "I have been divorced for five years, and I have been sending checks in my own name for much longer than that, and they are still sending material as though my husband is giving." Another woman remarked, "My husband was a trustee at a university, and every time we went up for dinner, his name card would say Mr. John P. and mine would say *Mrs. John* P. I kept saying, 'I'm *Mary* P.,' and I absolutely refused to wear a name tag." These thank-yous addressed to the husband when the wife had made a gift and failures to recognize the wife as a separate, and potentially generous, individual were most often cited as examples of inadequate recognition. Women are unforgiving about these errors and open in their advice to development practitioners on matters of traditional cultivation. As one woman commented:

We all know that women . . . hold the purse strings to a major percentage of money in the United States, and yet if I make a phone call to our local politician and my husband makes a phone call to our local politician, we all know who gets a phone call back first. I think this is a perfect example of why we as women are feeling the way we do. Of course, we want to see some control over the money we give. We don't feel like we've been very well accepted, or really appreciated, or even entertained the way men are. I don't know how many times my husband is taken to lunch by UCLA. In fact, if UCLA really wanted money, they'd spend a lot more time with me.

Wanting to see the results of giving

The women's desire to use wealth for philanthropic purposes during their own lifetimes was one of the more startling responses to questions regarding bequests and planned giving. A woman's need to know what she was able to accomplish with her philanthropy appeared stronger than the desire to accumulate wealth for the purpose of passing it on to the next generation. While all respondents expressed a sense of responsibility about providing for family members' needs, they favored an activist philanthropic role for themselves. In fact, what the women wanted most to pass on, as noted earlier, was a spirit of participation and generosity, the hallmarks of philanthropic behavior. Their desire for the transmission of values far exceeded their desire to bequeath wealth: "We actually believe that we're not really responsible for leaving our children a whole lot of money," said one woman. "What we are responsible for is leaving them a very good education with the understanding that they have to be productive human beings on this planet."

Responsibility to give

The responsibility to give is the final significant concept emphasized by all the women participants. It echoes through many other themes and discussions, from making a difference to educating future generations, and articulates an ethic prevalent among women philanthropists, whether they are giving their time, their money, or both. One woman recalled being "in a group of Soviet women about five years ago, and we went around the room and talked about how we got involved in the issues we were involved with, and we all said the same thing. We were all women between forty and fifty, feeling responsible for others." Like the responsibility for family and community that has historically belonged to women, the responsibility to give is a characteristic that cannot be underestimated in understanding women's philanthropic behavior.

Early results, future directions

The findings from the focus group study conducted by UCLA's Women and Philanthropy Program tell fundraisers that as philanthropists, or potential philanthropists, women may possess a variety of personal motivations and styles. Yet women are profoundly similar in certain respects: women want to be part of the process. They want plenty of information about the organization to which they donate, and they want to understand its programs. They want to be honored by having the request for a gift come from a person of rank and respect. They want to be courted. And, as they develop more and more sophistication, women expect to be offered membership on boards and to be sought out for positions of advisement.

One focus group member put it bluntly: "Get women involved in the process. Put us at the highest levels of planning. Put us on those boards. Give us the power and the responsibility that goes with giving the money." By using the vehicle of focus groups, the Women and Philanthropy Program has been able to bring women's voices to the university's development strategy discussions. Patterns of women's concerns, ranging from involvement to recognition, have been identified and can now be addressed. An eagerness for involvement in UCLA's programs has been noted, along with particular areas of interest, and development directors are now taking the next steps in cultivating individual women participants. Leaders have emerged, both as major donor prospects and volunteers, and we now have a small group of women who are viable candidates for trustee positions on the UCLA foundation board. Several women have been placed on dean's councils, and one is now chairing a program fundraising effort.

The most long-term contribution the focus groups have made to the university's development program, however, is the creation of a climate for women's giving. We have taken on the responsibility to listen and in doing so have begun to establish the trust that can make women comfortable in making large gifts. Even more importantly, we have brought together powerful women who now think of themselves as a group and who have expressed willingness to be educated further about both the university and philanthropy. For many, it is the first time they have examined their own philanthropic behavior; they want to continue their exploration, looking to the university and the activities we might offer as a starting point. Participation in a focus group also represents the first time many of the women have consciously identified themselves as philanthropists. Group discussions have created an intense and shared awareness, reminding us as development professionals that, indeed, philanthropists do not come to their role through a single act of generosity but rather through a long pattern of growth. We have initiated that growth in more than a few women; we now have the privilege and responsibility to sustain it.

One element in sustaining the growth of UCLA's women donors will be the direction of UCLA's Women and Philanthropy Program over the next few years. Two advisory task forces have been formed to help provide that direction: one is composed of nine philanthropists who participated in the focus group study and another consists of an equal number of UCLA development officers. Each task force is offering valuable suggestions about how the program might best serve both the university's development goals and its women donors.

Among the early suggestions from the philanthropists are activities such as financial planning seminars led by women professionals that address issues of specific interest to women, wider marketing of a women's health day currently conducted by members of the university's medical faculty, presentations by UCLA faculty whose work relates to women and leadership issues, and the formation of a group of donors with a particular interest in mentoring younger women and directing funds to areas of identified interest. The group's stated mission is to educate women to philanthropic behavior, to help them direct funds to areas of identified interest, and as a result, to provide support for the university's programs.

The development officers' task force helps the Women and Philanthropy Program focus on staff training issues and the establishment of individual cultivation and solicitation strategies. The task force has discussed with us the need for more data base work to better define women's giving and the ways in which planned giving can be incorporated into the program. Like its philanthropist counterpart, the development task force is interested in education that will move women along the learning curve for philanthropic behavior.

Along with sorting out the best ideas of the task forces and implementing them, the Women and Philanthropy Program is considering the design of a survey to reach an even larger number of UCLA's women. The focus group study will expand to a few more geographic areas outside Los Angeles, and the program alumnae will continue to play an active role in its development. Although these strategies emerged at a major public university, it is likely that they could also be used in other nonprofit settings.

Old stereotypes, new images

In her essay *A Room of One's Own*, Virginia Woolf imagines a sister for Shakespeare and admonishes, "She would come if we worked for her" (1929, p. 114). Like working for Shakespeare's sister, working for emerging women philanthropists in our own institutions means not only educating and listening and advocating but, most fundamentally, letting these women in. We must not, in conscious or unconscious ways, become like the beadle at the door of the Trinity College library, a "guardian angel barring the way with a flutter of black gown . . . a deprecating, silvery, kindly gentleman, who regretted in a low voice as he waved me back that ladies are only admitted to the library if accompanied by a Fellow of the College" (Woolf, 1929, pp. 7–8).

Long years of being locked out of the library creates, inevitably, a numbing effect upon the mind. Even after one is finally wandering among the stacks, there is bound to be a residue of insecurity. Action taken in this state tends to confirm as yet not fully disproved stereotypes of women as philanthropists: their gifts are smaller than we would like, often made tentatively, often with the modesty of anonymity. Their behavior stymies our efforts as development professionals and belies the fact that these women often have significant wealth at their disposal. But the wealth is not the issue. The stereotypes evolved during a time when a mother could still tell her daughter about the laws that once prohibited women from possessing the money they earned or inherited. The stereotypes remain true during a time in which discrepancies between men's and women's incomes still occur. The stereotypes have a context. And while society has moved to gradually eliminate that context, fundraisers cannot ignore its legacy. Women "need to be nurtured," a focus group participant told us, "because that's the way I would start out. . . . Then I would give more . . . then my sights would keep rising. I wasn't comfortable in the beginning with giving more. It's an experience. You have to learn to give."

Today women are learning how to give more in greater numbers. From Kathleen Dexter McCormick, whose farsighted gift of $2 million funded research that led to the development of the oral contraceptive, to Ellen Malcolm, founder of Emily's List, to Peg Yorkin, whose $10 million gift has endowed the Fund for the Feminist Majority, women are putting their money behind their beliefs. Motivational and stylistic differences between women and between women and men notwithstanding, fundraisers cannot afford to have women as anything less than equal partners.

References

Stone, K., and Sublett, D. "The UCLA Women and Philanthropy Focus Groups Report." Unpublished report. Office of Development, University of California, Los Angeles, 1992.

Woolf, Virginia. *A Room of One's Own.* Orlando, Fla.: Harcourt Brace Jovanovich, 1929.

DYAN SUBLETT *is a senior member of the development staff at the University of California, Los Angeles, where she codirects the Women and Philanthropy Program with Karen Stone.*

Advertisers have segmented their messages for years, and development professionals can borrow advertisers' methods to communicate with women prospects and donors. As the annual fund campaign at Saint Mary's College demonstrates, your own women constituents are one of your best research tools for creating these messages.

5

Women talking to women about giving: Creating incentives, avoiding resistance

Kaye Ferguson-Patton

DEVELOPMENT PROFESSIONALS are constantly looking for ways to broaden their donor bases and upgrade those donors who are presently giving to an institution. As donors are bombarded with more and more requests for voluntary dollars for increasingly greater needs, the competition for contributions grows more intense. Today, development professionals are placing a new emphasis on women as donors and as potential philanthropists. The target group of the 1990s is women, and the challenge is how to reach them most effectively. While the emphasis on women donors seems to be a recently discovered trend, there are organizations that have been successfully raising money from their female constituents for some time. These organizations are women's colleges,

NEW DIRECTIONS FOR PHILANTHROPIC FUNDRAISING, NO. 2, WINTER 1993 © JOSSEY-BASS PUBLISHERS

and they provide excellent examples of successful fundraising strategies. They have learned how to raise money from women by establishing new models for success that may be applicable to the entire nonprofit sector.

Targeting specific parts of your female constituency can yield more dollars for your institution. To develop the strategies that guide a program of specific targeting, you must borrow expertise learned from both the advertising industry and from recently studied communication trends between women. Such expertise is now being used to bring increasing success to colleges' annual fund programs.

A lesson from the advertising industry

As nonprofits seek to sophisticate their development efforts, they can take their cues from the marketing and advertising professionals who have honed target marketing to finite degrees. To understand how demographic targeting is accomplished, spend a few hours watching television, listening to the radio, or reading magazines in order to observe how advertisers talk to their customers. During this observation, it is worthwhile to switch stations and magazines frequently to expose your ear to a variety of formats and program styles aimed at different audiences. For example, it is unlikely that you will hear a commercial for an acne care product on an easy listening or classical music station. Similarly, it is unlikely that you will hear a commercial for senior citizen supplemental health insurance on a top forty rock-and-roll station or one that features heavy metal music. Magazines like *Modern Maturity* do not feature ads for bubble gum, and *Seventeen* is not apt to carry travel ads geared to retired adults.

Advertisers know that the high cost of media advertising means that they must select their media carefully, choosing those whose primary audience is at the right age and stage of life to be interested in the products the advertisers have to sell. Advertising agencies specialize in media placement services that deliver to the advertiser the potential customers most disposed to purchase the advertiser's product or service. The agencies also help advertisers craft and deliver the messages that appeal to the potential purchasers by reflecting the appropriate virtues of the product or service being sold.

Gender-specific advertising can also be part of the media mix and message developed by advertising experts. For example, cosmetic products purchased by women would not be advertised on a fishing show nor would fishing gear be advertised on a soap opera. However, the danger always exists of stereotyping the purchaser and/or the product and, as a result, ignoring potential customers. Therefore, astute marketers must be aware of who their customer actually is, how that customer can be reached, what messages will motivate that customer, and what messages or events will encourage repeat purchases of the product or service. Regularly studying one's audience and being sensitive to its needs and the messages to which it responds is part of successful marketing. Times, trends, and fads all influence customers' decisions.

Even apparently universal marketers segment their messages. For a prime example of the way this can be accomplished, watch the variety of McDonald's commercials that flood the television channels, and you will find that, with a little analysis, you can determine the age group that each one is designed to reach. As the consumers of McDonald's products have matured, the corporation has obviously made a concerted effort to reach each major age group. McDonald's ads show senior citizens enjoying a meal or grandparents bringing grandchildren in for a special lunch. Basketball teams come in to celebrate victories. Mothers bring in daughters; fathers bring in sons. Some ads even feature the senior citizens on the McDonald's work force. This range of messages represents targeted marketing at its zenith. McDonald's also advertises through a variety of media in order to capture and retain market segments.

Development applications

Advertisers' principles of target marketing can be integrated into development operations. A natural place to start is in direct-mail operations. Direct-mail solicitations can be among the most expensive programs in a development budget, so mailing specialized messages to specialized audiences is valid. Direct mail is also an area in which increased segmentation is possible through fundamental computer technology. It is hard to understand, then, why many development professionals avoid using the direct-mail expertise gained through the years by marketers. Development professionals will find that the following current examples from marketers provide information that can help fundraisers tailor their messages to specific constituencies in specific ways.

The most basic direct-mail model is a written message that states the case, gives an appealing example of the need, and then makes the "ask." Many institutions begin such letters with a "Dear Friends" salutation, produce the letters with the most inexpensive printing possible, and put them in window envelopes accompanied by some kind of response piece. A 1 percent return is considered outstanding. More sophisticated direct-mail models include personalized salutations and envelopes, letters produced on laser printers, and special letterheads designed for specific projects. These garner a better response. The more personalized the salutation and letter, the better the results fundraisers can expect. However, most organizations stop at the personalization of the salutation and tend to use a universal letter.

Other models get even more specific by asking in the text of the letter for an upgrade in the donation, stating the donor's past giving, and asking for a larger amount in the current year. Again, these letters have a personalized salutation, and some even repeat the person's name in the text of the letter. Special letters may also be written for giving-club members, with messages segmented by donor levels of giving. These models can be successful, and results can be further enhanced by targeting the messages by gender and by age. Such targeting for the future can increase a nonprofit's income from all solicitation media, including phonathons, person-to-person solicitations, and other fundraising campaign strategies. As development officers begin to understand the messages that relate to women differently from men and to younger donors differently from older donors, dialogues can also be tailored for these specific groups.

A case history of message identification

At Saint Mary's College in Notre Dame, Indiana, the information we use to segment our fundraising messages comes directly from our alumnae. Saint Mary's is a women's college with a history of nearly 150 years and a reputation as one of the top Roman Catholic women's colleges in the country (Council for Financial Aid to Education, 1992). Several events in the history of the college became relevant when we segmented our alumnae into age groups. For example, 50 percent of our alumnae graduated after 1972. Since then, a radical decrease has occurred in the number of women religious (that is, nuns) among the instructors. The geographic base of the student body has broadened, as has the diversity of the students. The curriculum has been kept current with trends in higher education, and such majors as home economics have been eliminated and more majors in mathematics and sciences added. The college's development professionals began to realize that the memories of the college among our older alumnae did not reflect the Saint Mary's of today. And they realized that the younger alumnae had little concept of what Saint Mary's was like thirty, forty, or more years ago. The historical changes in the college have contributed to these differing attitudes among the alumnae.

To garner a better sense of how these attitudes varied, the development staff took a very analytical look at letters written to classmates by volunteer alumnae in the reunion gift programs. The staff looked for common themes and verbiage. They also tried to

sort out the motivational messages involved in the parts of the letters that asked for a contribution. The results of this analysis
showed that alumnae who had graduated prior to 1972 seemed to
be steeped in nostalgia for the college and the relationship that
many of the alumnae had with the sisters who taught them. These
alumnae remembered their college years fondly. They also were on
campus at a time when no formal fundraising was done, and many
have no history of giving to the college. They are uncomfortable
talking about giving money. As one volunteer said of her class, "We
don't use the M-word when we talk about Saint Mary's. We were
taught that God will provide." Many of these older alumnae have
not revisited the campus in a number of years and, when they do,
are amazed at the number of new buildings and changes in the
"style" of the students, including the lack of uniforms and more
open visitation hours in the residence halls.

It is also notable that the majority of these alumnae have not had
careers, especially those who graduated prior to 1950. Among the
older group of graduates, then, the common theme seemed to be
to perpetuate the legacy of Saint Mary's College, its Catholic ori-
gins and traditions. Their nostalgic messages to their classmates
looked to the past rather than conveying a sense of the college's
current and future needs.

Among the women who graduated after 1972, the attitude was
quite different. Many are career oriented and are now entering the
most successful years of their careers. The exceptions are those
graduates of the past ten years who are still career building but who
have exceptional potential. The messages of these post-1972 graduates to each other tended to be more pragmatic about the future
of Saint Mary's. They were program oriented, with an emphasis on
what the graduates owe back to the college that helped them prepare for their career paths. They were concerned about the percentages of alumnae participation at Saint Mary's as compared to
other women's colleges, reflecting a competitive urgency. They
were concerned about the college's ability to provide to future generations the same kind of superior education that the recent grad-

uates felt they had received. Even the most recent graduates wrote messages that focused on college issues, in addition to acknowledging the reality of repaying student loans and trying to get their own careers started. For these alumnae, continued participation in the institution's future turned out to be key to their wanting to contribute to the annual fund campaign. In response to their perceived needs, the college has initiated a junior membership program in the giving clubs to bring these new alumnae recognition for those gifts that they can afford to give.

Establishing the model

In the following section, I will describe the basic steps that fundraisers need to take to establish a new model of cultivation and solicitation for their institutions, a model based on gender and age. Then I will show how Saint Mary's new model was developed and discuss some general implementation issues. This particular model is for a direct-mail program. At Saint Mary's, as the direct-mail program developed, it led the development planner into an integration of the direct-mail model with other modes of solicitation.

Stating the case

An institution's case statement serves the same purpose as the material that advertising executives refer to as a copy platform. It is a resource for developing specific messages geared to specific target markets. The fundamental data contained in the case statement can be molded to appeal to the targeted constituents that the organization hopes to reach: small donors, major donors, women, men, corporations, foundations, the general public, very specific publics, and other identifiable groups of internal and external constituents. In the certification course for development professionals, the National Society of Fundraising Executives defines the case statement as "a documentation of all information describing the facilities, budget, institutional plans, financial history, personnel, staff competence to serve the mission or the cause that the organization represents. It is a 'database'" (National Society of Fundraising Executives, 1986). The case should be a working document that can be written or presented in a variety of communication modes. It can be a brochure, a direct-mail piece, a speech, the platform for volunteer training, even a public service message. It must be communicated, ingested, and finally believed through as many methods as possible, including methods that will speak directly to the variety of women who represent part of the organization's constituency.

Target messages

The case is a variety of data base for a specific fundraising program, and that data base should include specific communication messages. For example, the result of the focus group study conducted by UCLA (see Chapter Four) is a data base that tells the university what its women constituents think about their roles as philanthropists. Similar focus groups and research conducted within the community of donors who give to your organization will provide valuable data for your case statement. Past files of women donors' letters to their peers will suggest the language and style you should use to tailor the case statement to each particular age group.

Identifying women donors' messages

Fundraisers can use several methods to identify the particular messages that women use when talking to each other about reasons for giving. The unbiased observations of the development professionals themselves are key to the identification of these messages. Methods can be as simple as reviewing volunteer letters and as complicated as specific focus group communication audits. Whatever the methodology used, the results will come from a compilation of data that shows where commonality exists among messages. Look for phrases commonly used by women in each age group and ask such questions as, How many of the writers are nostalgic? How many are concerned with the future of the nonprofit? How many are citing comparative data about similar organizations? What do the writers give as the primary reasons for giving? What language do they use to enlist their peers as donors?

Refining messages

Many articles written about women as donors and philanthropists cite major differences between the motivations of women and men. While still to be empirically tested, the supposition is that men will give to become involved, buying their way to the prestige and status of board membership, whereas women will seek to be involved first, and if they enjoy what they are doing and observing, they will then give to the organization. If the key for women is involvement first, then it definitely makes sense for development professionals to involve women donors in the testing and refinements of the targeted messages that have been gleaned for further study. There are three ways to accomplish this involvement:

1. Ask the volunteers to write sample drafts of letters that they feel would motivate them to give, featuring what is most important to them as donors about your organization and what they would say to other women their age. Be sure to identify for the volunteers the target group to whom they are writing so that they can give you their best effort.

2. Invite the volunteers to participate in a focus group where you can seek their reactions to several sample letters. The volunteers should discuss common messages and themes in the letters, indicate whether they respond favorably or unfavorably to the messages and themes, and describe what they would change. Use the same opportunity to discuss which graphics and colors they find most appealing. Have simple graphic layouts for them to view and respond to in the group setting.

3. As a control to the focus groups, select some individuals to review and respond to the same materials. However, do not be alarmed if some individual reviewers are poles apart from the focus groups. A researcher may often have to disregard opinions that are far afield from the average response.

Implementing findings

At Saint Mary's College, our implementation of our findings about our alumnae involved development of three distinct pieces for our annual fund mailings. The first, for those who graduated prior to 1972, featured a nostalgic theme, with soft graphics and copy that reflected their fond memories of the college. The second, for those who graduated after 1972, had crisper graphics and more straightforward copy, which emphasized the future of the college and stressed the importance of participation percentages. The third piece, which went to the reunion-year alumnae, was a combination of the two pieces but leaned more heavily on the nostalgic copy and graphics than on the future-oriented piece.

Volunteer training

After appropriate messages are identified, be sure to incorporate them into the volunteer fundraiser training sessions. Women are eager to be armed for success in their solicitations. At Saint Mary's, the sharing of these targeted messages has proven to be interesting, motivating, and facilitating for the volunteers exposed to the information in the messages.

Staff training

Perhaps the most productive use of information about the targeted groups is in the training of the staff who will make solicitations and work to facilitate the success of the volunteers. Once the staff understand the differences in the messages, they can more successfully bring calls to closure and build on the success of their volunteers.

Informing graphic artists and copywriters

If the organization uses graphic artists and copywriters, they too need to share in the information gleaned from the volunteer message writers and focus groups. Then, and only then, can they amplify the messages and translate them into the best possible vehicles for garnering more and larger gifts, whether those vehicles be printed materials, video presentations, or public service announcements.

Informing administrators

Often development professionals can forget this important group of solicitors. The nonprofit organization's administrators need to be fully informed and sold on the concept of the target marketing approach to fundraising. Once they understand the concept and the messages, the administrators can spread the messages in the course of their communications with donors and potential donors.

Importance of strategy

The movement of people who are new, small donors up the ladder to becoming major donors and, finally, to leaving wealth in the form of planned gifts and/or bequests does not just happen. Development officials should lay out the whole process in a marketing strategy. This strategy should include the targeting of various donor constituencies, and the women in the donor base of any institution should be a targeted group. While such targeting may be easier for an educational institution, the concept can be applied to other types of nonprofits.

A marketing strategy is a map for accomplishment of the development objectives. It involves more than the development officer's taking in the disciplines of public relations, alumni relations, research and information gathering, volunteer management, direct-mail solicitations, and telemarketing (Kotler and Andreason, 1987). By employing sound target marketing strategies, the development office can answer the needs of an institution by matching them with the needs of the donors—women and/or men—and motivating the levels of donor support that can ensure the institution's future.

Given a valid and value-laden case for supporting the mission of the nonprofit institution or organization and the promise of involvement in reaching that mission, potential volunteers and donors are more likely to respond. Effective campaigns can be devised to meet institutional needs, and appeals can be tailored to trigger positive responses from women donors. How development professionals talk to their women donors is a vital part of achieving a positive response. Women donors are not the same as male donors. Development professionals must talk women donors' language and must meet them at the point at which they are willing to support the institution. Development professionals must *know* their female constituencies and research them thoroughly to know not only what they are capable of giving but what will motivate them to give, whether they are first-time annual fund donors or the multimillion-dollar major donor.

Sharing segmentation and marketing information with your staff and volunteers is key to facilitating their success. All donors may be created equal, but the messages that motivate them to give are not. Know what moves your potential donors to give and then help solicitors send them that message to gain optimal results. Education of the development staff is key, and your women donors themselves are your best teachers.

References

Council for Financial Aid to Education. *Voluntary Support of Education, 1991.* New York: Council for Financial Aid to Education, 1992.

Kotler, P., and Andreason, A. R. *Strategic Marketing for Nonprofit Organizations.* (3rd ed.) Englewood Cliffs, N.J.: Prentice Hall, 1987.

National Society of Fundraising Executives. Material from survey course, 1986.

KAYE FERGUSON-PATTON *is vice president of college relations at Saint Mary's College in Notre Dame, Indiana, and has twenty years' experience in marketing, advertising, and broadcasting.*

*To encourage attention to women donors in a coed-
ucational environment, fundraisers must have
focus and commitment. A program at Colgate
University identifies some suggestions and first
steps.*

6

Starting a new program at your institution

Ronald A. Joyce, Tracy West Barlok

IN APRIL 1992, it was reported that in the previous decade women
had outnumbered men in undergraduate enrollments. Moreover,
the report said, "when they graduate, women are marrying later,
having fewer children and pursuing professional careers in medi-
cine, law and engineering" (McMillen, 1992, p. A32). As women's
roles have shifted from "bread bakers" to "bread winners," women
have become equal partners in decisions about family financial
matters. Women's longevity compared to men also suggests that
they may have more opportunities than men to make decisions
about philanthropic distributions (see Chapter One). Hillary
Smith, director of development for the Haymarket People's Fund,
spoke to the same issue when she commented that "women are now
taking on leadership roles and changing the face of traditional philanthropy. Older white men historically donated philanthropically. . . . That's all changing as more women get control over
money" (Teltsch, 1992, p. B6).

NEW DIRECTIONS FOR PHILANTHROPIC FUNDRAISING, NO. 2, WINTER 1993 © JOSSEY-BASS PUBLISHERS

As evidence emerges that increasing numbers of women are making significant contributions to charitable organizations, some nonprofit institutions are beginning to analyze the benefits of the growing economic clout of women. Yet many other nonprofit institutions, including colleges, are not yet taking notice of this new dimension of philanthropic activity, and a continuing relative absence of both hard data and anecdotal information confirms the thesis that women are still an untapped reservoir of philanthropic involvement and support.

Colgate's survey of programs

Anticipating that tailoring a special program aimed at the cultivation and solicitation of women as donors and volunteers might be an important first step in realizing women's philanthropic potential, Colgate University development staff embarked upon a survey to learn what had worked elsewhere and who was really paying attention to this new breed of donor. In phone interviews and field visits with many nonprofit organizations, we found that very few have researched and developed a plan to better involve their female constituents as donors and volunteers.

While the role models among educational institutions that have educated both women and men are startlingly few, some merit mention. In just six years after the University of Pennsylvania established its Trustee Council of Penn Women, that council has emerged as a powerful organization for women's issues and has raised millions of dollars from Penn women. Council director Sharon Hardy says that the formation of the council has enabled Penn "to attract women who really had no interest in Penn and they've become excited about giving. . . . It's also a great way to uncover prospects" (telephone conversation with the author, February 1993). Cornell University established its President's Council of Cornell Women about three years ago. Director Martha Eller says that the council began as a board to advise the president about important women's issues. The 125-member organization is divided into subcommittees, including one that focuses specifically on development and financial support for projects that influence the quality of life for women on the Cornell campus. The college expects—and has already experienced—a growth in its gifts.

Karen Stone, Dyan Sublett, and their development colleagues at UCLA have researched their alumnae and major gift prospects and are beginning to build a program that merges the interests of these graduates with the needs of the institution (see Chapter Four). The report they filed on their 1992 focus groups and their conclusions of their early studies should be required reading for all fundraising practitioners (Stone and Sublett, 1992). The University of Wisconsin, which has established a program to focus on women's giving, has used focus group techniques, and a three-year training model has realized significant successes in its efforts to target women donors.

Yet research about programs at smaller coed institutions—especially those that were single-sex institutions just twenty to twenty-five years ago—provides a stunning surprise. Few are giving special attention to women, despite their acknowledging that the average gift from their women donors is generally a small fraction of the average gift from men. Many of these schools are only just beginning to recognize that there are real benefits beyond gift support that will accrue to those places that reach out to women. The record to date at most schools is abysmal, even at those institutions that are national leaders in total giving.

Until recently, Colgate University was included in that large group that has not yet taken advantage of the giving and volunteer potential of its alumnae. Pressed by the need to be more competitive in the philanthropic marketplace and recognizing that we were not giving our women graduates the opportunity or incentive to make a real difference at our institution, we decided to start a program of philanthropy for Colgate alumnae. The decision represented pure institutional self-interest. We had women of talent and persuasion who were capable of assuming leadership roles in mobilizing interest and support for their alma mater. Our analyses indicated that we were not reaching them in meaningful ways.

We cite our own institution here for two reasons. First, we at Colgate University seem to be slightly ahead of many of our development colleagues in our trial-and-error development of a new program. Perhaps our longer learning curve can shorten someone else's. Also, until recently, we have had a traditional male-oriented fundraising program. We hope others will see aspects of themselves in us and be moved to action.

Women's involvement

An all-male institution at its founding in 1819, Colgate was a liberal arts college where young men were taught by men, and male values dominated. Women were first accepted as undergraduates in 1970, and Colgate now has nearly 5,000 alumnae—about 20 percent of all graduates. Today we graduate an equal number of women and men.

A 151-year-old bachelor has a hard time breaking habits. Men still occupy the majority of leadership and administrative positions on the campus, and women number only five of thirty-one positions on the board of trustees. Just a quarter of the tenured full-time faculty are now women. Increasingly, however, women's involvement has improved. Our alumni corporation's new president is a woman, as is its executive director. Nearly one-quarter of the alumni corporation's board of directors are women. Class fundraisers and alumni club presidents nationwide represent a proportionally larger share of women than there are in the alumni body as a whole. In coeducational classes, the donor participation rates of alumnae tend to be equal to or better than men's, yet the average gift for alumnae is one-fifth that for men. In the university's leadership support group of 1,200 members, only 22 are women. Indeed, of the nearly 8,000 graduates identified as rated prospects in our development data base, only 175 are women. As it is, we believe the recent data undervalue the number of alumnae prospects and their giving potential.

In 1995, Colgate will celebrate twenty-five years of coeducation. Anticipation of that anniversary has given us reason to pause and reflect on the various ways women have enhanced the institution. Given the data we have just cited, and the growing national phenomena of women as donors and influencers, our conclusion was obvious: the status quo was unacceptable and perhaps even dangerous. We needed a better way to incorporate our alumnae in the many aspects of our external relations program.

Development of Colgate's women donors program

It can be difficult for an institution to look back and chart its own first course of action on a new development program. In our experience, the determination to develop our new program came from a conviction that women are taking a new and very powerful role in philanthropy. It is essential for development officers to assess how their institutions' programs can respond to this emerging opportunity. Certainly development officers will need the support of institutional leaders to overcome decades of neglect and inertia. Colgate is fortunate to have President Neil Grabois, who, influenced by his own intuition and recent articles in the media, began to push for action. He was joined by a leading trustee, Lorie Slutsky, one of the college's earliest woman graduates and president of the New York Community Trust, the largest community program of its kind. Indeed, when she was elected as the trust's new president in 1988, it was seen as a move that challenged stereotypes about leadership and power in the world of philanthropy. Now, as a national spokesperson for philanthropy, she has special insights and perspectives about those who are emerging as makers and grantors of wealth in the next generation, and she commands special respect on Colgate's board of trustees. In this case, the coalition of a president and a leading trustee guaranteed positive action.

The impetus for new ways of doing business with women, especially in smaller charitable organizations, can best come when effective partnerships are formed between staff and volunteer leaders.

Program direction and goals

The next step is determining the direction in which to take the program and how to proceed once that direction is chosen. Currently there are few program models to follow and even those may not approximate the condition and environment your planning faces. Still, it is best to avail yourself of the growing body of information that does exist and to make contacts with professional colleagues who are actively engaged in making similar changes. Each organization and institution, once committed to the notion of making fundamental changes in how it wishes to relate to women, must stake out long-term goals and develop a supporting schedule to determine the destination it wants to reach and how it will arrive at various stages along the way.

Using the twenty-fifth anniversary of women students at Colgate as a benchmark moment, we determined certain preliminary targets, among them specific increases in the percentage of giving among women, increases in their average yearly gifts, and growth in the numbers of women in various leadership giving groups. In addition, we set goals for new levels of alumnae involvement on the board of trustees and in a variety of fundraising and friend-raising leadership positions. Most importantly, we made strong commitments and set aggressive goals for the number of personal field visits by development officers and the college president that we would hold with our women graduates. None of these ambitions was irreversibly fixed. We recognized early on that new information and new conditions might cause us to change our view of where we ought to be headed. Yet we remained convinced that nonspecific goals would be too easy to ignore. We felt there was value in putting pressure on ourselves to stretch and to reach. We wanted accountability, in part because it emphasized the priority we were giving our alumnae. We also repeatedly underscored the fundamental principle of our work: Colgate University is making a permanent commitment to women as donors and volunteers. Accepting anything less than that as our purpose would disable the program.

Even before we began to look outside for volunteer help, we made an important inside decision: one person would have direct program responsibility, and we would allocate appropriate time and resources. The dean and the development vice president supported those decisions. The selection of a designated program director confirmed our seriousness of purpose internally and externally. We felt that any division of labor that failed to put one person in charge would dilute our effort. That the director selected was a well-regarded, senior-level person was another example of Colgate's commitment.

Program resources

Institutional resources vary dramatically, but it is sufficient to say that the program needs adequate funding to succeed. What is adequate will be a local determination, but one that should be considered with care. We also recommend that you follow the example of Penn, Cornell, Colgate, and others by forming a women's council or advisory group with a direct link to your president or board. There are various views about this group's optimal size and how structured or informal it should be; your own circumstances will determine these answers. A representative cadre of women can provide a wealth of experience, understanding, and advice that will be invaluable in shaping and reaching program goals. Such a group can also give important public validation and status to your program. The group becomes a support system essential to handling the growing pains of doing something new but important.

Learning about women donors

Obviously it is important to meet and understand your female constituency. You will learn early on that they are excited to be asked for their opinions. You may also learn how quickly word of your enterprise will reach other interested people. Nicki Tanner, cochair of the recent Wellesley College campaign, has said that Wellesley's campaign dialogue dinners with alumnae were extremely important on this front: "We took their responses, suggestions, questions, and concerns seriously; we valued them. And because this is still a rare experience for women in our society, they said thank you—with great generosity" (Hall, 1992b, p. 1).

Focus groups are an extremely important source of information for program development. They have the advantage of tapping into a network of women who have been waiting a very long time to express their views and concerns. These sessions cultivate a better understanding of the needs of your organization among donors, help you evaluate the strengths and weaknesses of your program, and assist you in redefining your goals and objectives. They also lead to some positive actions among participants, including increases in gift giving and greater willingness to become involved as a volunteer. Volunteers make good donors: involvement leads to commitment and commitment leads to support.

After collecting data from your sessions, you may begin to notice trends in donors' and prospective donors' attitudes about your organization. Borrowing from the UCLA model (see Chapter Four), Colgate has begun organizing focus groups for its women graduates. The information we have learned from our early discussion groups confirms many of the UCLA findings about women's reactions to fundraising appeals and how we should ask alumnae for gifts. Many of Colgate's alumnae said they give not to support the status quo but to effect change. In 1993 focus sessions, we heard such comments as these: "An appeal to me is more meaningful when specific needs are identified." "People would give more gifts if they knew where their dollars were going." "Giving is tied back to my personal experiences. I want to help develop things I am interested in. . . . I want to give to specific programs because I know they need that help."

One-on-one staff visits with key women donors and prospects will complement your focus sessions. This personal approach can serve the same informal goal as the focus groups, but the intimacy of the meeting can add to both the donors' and the staff's depth of knowledge in particular areas. These visits often help to develop bonds and loyalties that can be drawn on later in organizing volunteer assignments and solicitations. Male development officers have used such cultivation approaches with male prospects for some time. Although women also value personal contact and relationships, at many places most women have not received this kind of attention and respect.

Reviewing and revising goals and assessing progress

Once data are gathered and analyzed, a program should be ready to move to the next stage. This may be an appropriate time for you to formalize and enlarge the advisory group or council. In turn, that group may want to review the initial set of long-term program goals, integrating the new information into a revised set of goals and operating style.

Few schools we know have progressed to this stage. Our women's advisory committee and on-campus leadership have reviewed focus sessions transcripts and are beginning to formulate new program ideas for career mentoring and networking for women—one issue that was of great concern to our alumnae. Our ambition is to be well positioned by program reputation and personal relationships to begin the actual solicitation of leadership gifts from women at the public announcement of our next campaign. As mentioned earlier, we have also set goals for increasing the number of women in our leadership donor club and for increasing the average gift of alumnae in the coming year. Our other goals include the formation of an on-campus committee to address the involvement and solicitation of women athletes and of women in specific academic areas. We plan to define new giving opportunities to match the interests and aspirations of women donors and are even considering the development of a gender-specific gift stewardship program. How we credit, thank, and recognize women for their gifts and volunteer efforts will require a new sensitivity and style.

Along the way, it is important to give strong publicity to your program, using publications to feature not only the program but also the donors and volunteers who are setting examples. Based on what you learn from volunteers, you may want to develop special leadership training programs and conferences for women to update them on your organization's needs. We anticipate that the next major benchmark for review and analysis of the program at Colgate will occur at the end of the program's third year. By then, data will show whether participation rates and average gifts by women have improved. We expect leadership support from women to increase, and we suspect that our knowledge of our alumnae, specifically those who have greater giving capacities, will improve. At this stage of the Colgate program, we know what we want, but we do not yet know what to expect. We understand that time and patience are important requirements and long-term cultivation of women donors is necessary. Lessons learned from other aspects of our development efforts suggest that commitment and continuity are essential to program success, especially in the first three years. Some skeptics will be watching to see if the program continues to receive priority attention. Is there follow-through? Are promises kept? Is there a change in the college's traditional behavior? Will the goals and ambitions of alumnae be respected and supported by the institution?

As with any new program, we expect turbulence. Not all women or men will embrace the special attention and resources focused on women. We have already learned that many of our women graduates have been feeling disenfranchised for so long that they have no interest in building new relationships with the university. We know that we will have to remain flexible within the general guidelines of our program. Still we expect to succeed. We hope other charitable organizations can learn from our successes and failures. There will be both, but we are convinced that the net results of our efforts will empower Colgate women and improve our institution.

Many Colgate alumnae have never been asked to give, certainly not in a personal way, especially by people they know and respect.

We suspect that other colleges' alumnae are not much different from Colgate's in this respect. But we have begun to recognize that there are differences in the way men and women should be approached and how they respond to requests for their financial support and time commitment. There is too much at stake for us to remain unresponsive to those differences. While working to meet our own needs and challenges, we hope our experiences will also encourage and shape other charities to stretch and reach.

References

Hall, H. "Female Leaders Encourage Expanded Efforts to Increase Charitable Giving by Women." *Chronicle of Philanthropy*, Nov. 3, 1992a, p. 10.

Hall, H. "Women's New Charity Clout." *Chronicle of Philanthropy*, June 16, 1992b, p. 1.

McMillen, L. "College Fund Raisers See Their Alumnae as Untapped Donors." *Chronicle of Higher Education*. Apr. 1, 1992, pp. A31–A32.

Stone, K., and Sublett, D. "The UCLA Women and Philanthropy Focus Groups Report." Unpublished report. Office of Development, University of California, Los Angeles, 1992.

Teltsch, K. "Shaking Up Old Ways of Benevolence." *New York Times*, Sept. 15, 1992, pp. B1, B4, B6.

RONALD A. JOYCE *is vice president for alumni affairs, communications, and development at Colgate University.*

TRACY WEST BARLOK *was Colgate University's first female alumni director and is now director of Colgate's special gift programs.*

The University of Wisconsin empowers women philanthropically by giving them the skills to seek support. A plan that started with focus groups and developed into a structured training program to empower women as donors and effective solicitors has had an excellent effect at the university and is a model for others.

7

Training women volunteers to seek major gifts

Martha A. Taylor

AT THE END OF THE LAST CENTURY, some women became active philanthropists on both local and national levels, responding to the needs and opportunities of society. Important charitable organizations were formed and women participated effectively in the organizations' work and had an impact in changing society. Recognition of these women's philanthropic impact is just beginning (see, for example, Fisher, 1991; McCarthy, 1990). The last decade of the twentieth century could see an even more effective role for women in the U.S. philanthropic arena if both institutional attitudes and approaches to women donors are changed. Changes in the traditional and hierarchical operating procedures within development offices may also be necessary if these offices are to attract and retain women as significant players in charitable institutions. Sensitizing development officers to women's needs and interests is an

NEW DIRECTIONS FOR PHILANTHROPIC FUNDRAISING, NO. 2, WINTER 1993 © JOSSEY-BASS PUBLISHERS

important part of these officers' training. Because development officers' time and influence are limited, education of volunteers is essential in fundraising. One of the most effective ways to raise funds is to have trained volunteers solicit major gifts. Women volunteers who have been philanthropically active can effectively motivate their peers to contribute major gifts also. Philanthropist Helen Hunt stated another reason for training women volunteers when she declared, "I always prefer to be asked for a gift by a woman."

In this chapter, I will emphasize how a structured training program that is sensitive to women's values can be used to train women to solicit major gifts. When the fundraisers' goal is also to influence women to consider major gifts, formal training can be complemented by other forms of participation in the institution. For example, a donor and solicitor can be asked to serve as an ongoing "advocate" and/or as a "reference" for an organization to other potential donors. Traditionally, men have been involved as the volunteers in the solicitation process, and major gifts officers, with the exception of those at women's colleges and organizations, have also called upon more men than women. For many charities, the simple step of having solicitors call upon women in proportion to women's representation on the prospect list would substantially increase the number of major donors who are women.

Volunteer advocates

At the University of Wisconsin, we believe that, for women, both involvement and inclusion are special forms of affirmation that can also be inducements to active philanthropy. The implications of this idea are that the professional practitioner should find means to engage volunteers and potential donors in the institution and its fundraising so that these donors' inclusion and engagement will support philanthropy. Your asking a woman if she will serve as an advocate for her area of interest permits her to become an example for other women and encourages their involvement. If she prefers to avoid publicity, ask her if you can use her as an example only when you are talking to other women considering a similar gift. In other words, ask her to serve as a reference for your organization. Assuming that women enjoy sharing their experiences and being part of a group, the donor will actually enjoy describing her own rationale for giving to a potential donor.

It is often difficult for women who have given a major gift to accept widespread public recognition. Philanthropist Maddie Glazer of Des Moines, Iowa, has described the feeling of isolation that she experiences from other women concerning publicity about her $6 million gift to Drake University (personal communication, 1992). Development officers value people who are willing to pose as role models, and they often think in terms of public acclaim for such donors. However, since many women seem to want to avoid the distancing from their peers that publicity may engender, fundraisers must permit women, when necessary, to serve as role models without public acclaim. For men, recognition tells the world they have done well. For a woman, it may set her apart from her community. As a first step, you can ask the woman major donor to serve as a public example, and if she says no, you can ask if she will serve as a reference. Often, she will be comfortable as a reference for another woman considering a major gift. You can then tell other prospects you visit about what Jane Doe has done, and explain that Jane would be happy to talk to the prospects about it.

A second role for a donor to play is advocate, that is, informal spokesperson for your organization. Ask her to refer potential supporters to you and then move her past the referrals to actually asking, informally, for a gift. The definition of a formal solicitation sometimes scares women away from the process, but a woman who is unwilling to serve on a formal committee may want to know whether a friend is participating as a major donor. It is possible for fundraisers to maintain donor confidentiality while also linking women by having one ask another to attend an event or participate as her guest. This way, even though the process of cultivation and solicitation is not formalized, the donor still engages in that process. While she may not be the person to close the request for a gift, the donor has become an activist in the gift solicitation process and through her own enthusiasm has helped advance that gift.

An advocate can help you by being prepared to say good words about your organization in other settings. If someone criticizes the organization, your donor can speak to that person's concern, or if the donor does not know how to respond to the allegation, she can seek out the answer and get back to the person with information. Volunteers recommend that they also act as advocates by talking about the exciting activities they enjoy when they are involved with an organization. Encouraging volunteers to talk about your charity with enthusiasm is a simple step that can improve the responses your organization receives from others. Every major woman donor should be asked to serve as an advocate. Once she does, she can more easily make the transition to a more formal training process and to the skills necessary for effective solicitation.

Attributes of formal training

Our experience in implementing a volunteer solicitation training program at University of Wisconsin suggests that it is well to consider the attributes that are discussed in the following sections. Empirical testing may show that these attributes always apply to women's philanthropy (Fisher, 1991).

Women like the collaborative process

Because women enjoy collaborating, suggest ideas and concepts to your women donors, but provide a flexible environment that will enable your leaders and your volunteer groups to conceptualize their own philosophy of giving. Focus groups that include new volunteers or prospective volunteers have proved an effective way to allow women to participate in shaping philanthropic endeavors. These groups give women donors an opportunity to be heard, to share experiences, and to create the direction for a program. Focus groups can be the means through which women begin their philanthropic empowerment (Stone and Sublett, 1992). Women seek to be part of the process that establishes procedures and programs to fit their specific interests. They enjoy brainstorming and discussing ideas that can help establish group consensus. This experience encourages women both to envision and to plan in a collaborative way; thus, it is important to provide an opportunity for such participation and the flow of ideas early in the process.

Women like to work in groups

Women enjoy getting together to talk about mutual concerns and to connect with those who share their interests. Traditionally, women's groups have chosen special events as a way of raising money, events that allowed women to collaborate in their raising of funds and provided a focus through which women could establish connections with both others and the cause. It is critical to build on women's desire for collaboration and connection in both your orientation and training process (Fisher, 1991).

Women view each other as peers

Women may be more likely than men to be willing to accept a spectrum of socioeconomic levels among the people who make solicitations from them. In general, your prospects should be visited by a carefully selected team of volunteers and staff. Volunteers involved should be selected for their own giving record or relationship to the prospect. And while women appear to be less status conscious than men about the individual who cultivates and solicits them and more concerned about the individual's commitment to the cause and relationship to the prospective donor, without evidence from empirical research, we can only suggest that women may respond better to a friend or acquaintance than to a stranger, regardless of the socioeconomic status of the friend compared to that of the stranger. How this correlates with men's peer-to-peer volunteer and solicitation work has yet to be tested. A high-level career woman in a professionally facilitated focus group at UCLA commented that "peer pressure turns me off" (Dyan Sublett, personal communication to author, 1992). Women prospects seem to be especially accepting of younger women who solicit them, recognizing that the younger women's circumstances are necessarily different from their own. Women prospects appear to be more willing than men to rate the importance of a volunteer's gift by its relationship to the volunteer's means rather than by its actual size. The relationship between the volunteer's and the prospective donor's abilities to give does not appear to be critical to the success of the call, but this too has yet to be tested. Some donor-solicitors seem especially to enjoy meeting new women from different backgrounds. They view this opportunity as a special benefit in the cultivation and solicitation process. Major gift solicitations assume that the donor has a certain level of means and that the donor's philanthropy has the potential to affect change. Such solicitations merit a high level of sensitivity and attention. Yet it appears that women will bring to the solicitation process fewer conscious hierarchical concerns and more attention to the issues of connection and the cause itself. Consequently, any training program for women should include this emphasis in its approach.

In all development work, it continues to be essential that the volunteer solicitor have demonstrated her own conviction, commitment, and potential comparable to her means before she solicits another.

A formal training program

Although yet to be fully tested empirically, the foregoing considerations about women donors are central to the formal training program designed for the University of Wisconsin Foundation's Council on Women's Giving. The combination of these considerations and a strategically staged training process are having an impact, and each stage, or session, of the university's program has helped the university to engage more women in the philanthropic process.

First program session

The first session of the program teaches women volunteers the following information:

- The motivations for giving and the basic concept that major gifts come from personal face-to-face contacts.

- Suspected differences between men's and women's attitudes toward philanthropy and how both cultivation and solicitation techniques might differ for men and for women because of these differences.

- The details of the solicitation call itself, including the listening skills and props that aid solicitors in making the first call, the detailed steps of the fundraising process from cultivation to close, and communication tools that overcome objections.

- The projects and needs of the institution, presented in detail and including institutional management and finances.

- Types of giving, including planned giving.

- Personal examples of giving, including testimonials and personal presentations by donors themselves or the volunteers or staff working with specific donors.

Second program session

This training session was held during a two-hour lunch one month after the first training session. The purpose of the second session was to review the major gift process and do more work on the specifics of a call. At this and subsequent training sessions, a faculty member presented details of specific opportunities for giving at the

university. Our experience has shown that women seek more details about the project they wish to fund than men and may want to
assume more accountability for how the gift is allocated to the
project. Philanthropist Pleasant Rowland, president of Pleasant
Company, a $60-million firm that sells high-quality dolls and ac-
cessories, mainly to women, also says that "women want the big
picture, and all the details to fill in the big picture. They want to
see the specifics." Rowland adds, "As the president of my own foundation, I find many of the proposals I receive to be without the details [I need to] relate to the project. Universities [also] fail to gain
women's attention . . . because they don't give out the specifics
about projects up front. They are vague [when] getting an appointment, saying they want to explore [the women's] areas of interest and [then] give them the specifics. The universities have a
real need for gifts, but they haven't learned yet how to attract more
women [who can make] major gifts, . . . because of their approach"
(Pleasant Rowland, personal communication at a meeting, Octo-
ber 1992). The information provided to the volunteers at the second session was not only for their use in their solicitations but was
intended to assist the volunteers to evaluate projects that would be
worthy of their own support.

After the university presentation, calling techniques were
demonstrated through role-playing. We have used role-playing
consistently in major gift training sessions for both men and
women. Kit Saunders Nordeen, the cochair of the University of
Wisconsin Foundation's Council on Women's Giving, explains
that "In this all-female context, you can create a sense of collegial-
ity among [your group] through role-playing." Nordeen notes that
"one of the most successful formats [for role-playing has been] the
humorous 'wrong' call to . . . set the women at ease." Three members of the committee then present a "good" call, and the group
then critiques each of the role-plays.

Pairing volunteer solicitors with the right prospects was a major
task that required a lot of attention. The committee received the

list of prospects at the second training session, and then returned their selections from the list plus the names of additional people they wished to contact. Again, because we allowed flexibility in the process, the women who were willing to share their own experiences with a prospect but who did not wish to choose names themselves for individual calls could ask to work with another volunteer or staff member. Some women identified prospects to call on within the next month; others took six months to a year. At each subsequent meeting, the list of contacts and volunteers assigned was distributed. The cochairs and staff made many follow-up calls and held some individual meetings with a few women concerning their assignments.

Third program session

This training, held one month after the second session, focused on the university's needs. A faculty member described a specific project, and then a detailed financial report was distributed for reference. A senior University of Wisconsin Foundation staff member, who is a woman, gave an overview of the administration and management of funds received and of endowment management. Finally, women on the committee gave testimonials about why they gave their gifts. Motivation for giving was stressed. These testimonials were moving, inspirational, and one suspects, effective catalysts for other donors. The cochairs began the testimonials, others were asked to comment, and it appeared that the women spoke from their hearts about their lives and values. Sharing these experiences was both encouraging and instructive.

Fourth program session

The fourth session was a one and one-half hour presentation by an expert on planned giving who reviewed the major planned-giving vehicles and their tax ramifications. In addition to learning to speak about planned giving to donor prospects, the volunteer solicitors learned about giving vehicles they might use themselves.

Sustaining the training

Following the four training sessions, the Council on Women's Giving met monthly and then every two months to keep the momentum moving. The monthly meetings included updates on progress and contacts volunteers had made, reports on specific projects or programs at the university and the value of private support for those projects, reports and testimonials from individual members on their gifts, and anecdotes about other donors' participation and support. The shared collaboration and indications of progress reinforced the women's involvement.

Early program results

One initial result of the training program was that calls made by volunteer solicitors upon current givers for additional support resulted in some immediate gifts. Personal contacts that Council volunteers made with prospects who did not yet have a relationship with the university are likely to result in future donors. A long-term fundraising philosophy was clearly understood by the women who participated in the training; they recognized that true relationships take years to nurture.

Participants also learned the need to conquer (and how to conquer) their anxieties stemming from their lack of familiarity with the major gift solicitation process. These meetings stimulated the building and nurturing of friendships and relationships. The Council members appreciated the investment the University of Wisconsin Foundation made in them through the training process, and learned that the university valued them as a part of the institution. They learned skills that will help the university to raise funds for current and future projects, projects that reflect values. By the end of the training program, the volunteers knew that enlisting the support of another gives that person a great opportunity to experience the pleasure of giving.

At the end of the Council's first training program, twenty-eight women had made about three donor contacts each; this was the first time they had ever done this. During the first year, more than thirty major donors were recruited at a minimum of $10,000 each. Two estate plans totalling more than $250,000 each have been written as a direct result of the calls. Additional major gifts were given by prospects who attended the cultivation events or who were referred to a staff member by women present. As with any committed group of volunteers, some of the best donors were the council members, and many increased their support or started new funds as a result of their council program experience.

These volunteers became some of our institution's best advocates because they perceived themselves to be part of the institutional family. Further, they demonstrated an understanding, determination, and enthusiasm that inspired the professional development officers. A synergy between staff and volunteers was created that encouraged personal values and a true philanthropic spirit to emerge on behalf of the projects. Our effort to enable women to be more active philanthropists has benefited both them and the university. It also provides a model for the involvement and training of other potential philanthropists by other institutions.

References

Fisher, J. Speech to the Council on Women's Giving, Forum on Women and Philanthropy, Madison, Wis., June 26, 1991.

Hunt, H. Remarks at the annual Payne, Forrester & Olsson client seminar, September 17, 1992.

McCarthy, K. D. *Lady Bountiful Revisited: Women, Philanthropy, and Power.* New Brunswick, N.J.: Rutgers University Press, 1990.

Stone, K., and Sublett, D. Discussion at the meeting of the National Network of Women as Philanthropists, San Francisco, March 1992.

MARTHA A. TAYLOR *is vice president of the University of Wisconsin Foundation and cofounder of the National Network of Women as Philanthropists.*

Efforts to focus philanthropic resources on women's special needs and to empower women of all socioeconomic and multicultural groups as philanthropists have created a rapidly growing complex of women's foundations and federations committed to funding, educating, training, and advocating to meet the needs of women donors, philanthropists, and grant recipients.

8

By women, for women: The women's funding movement

Susan Church, Carol Mollner

OVER THE PAST TWENTY-FIVE YEARS, women's efforts to achieve and sustain equity under the law, in the workplace, in education, and in society have been accompanied by a reexamination of women's role in the nonprofit sector. This third wave of the women's movement in the United States has included challenges to many of the historical assumptions about how and why women become and remain volunteers, donors, and/or employees of nonprofit organizations. Among the most interesting of these challenges has been the establishment of more than sixty women's funds in the United States, along with at least two in Canada. The reasons for the growth of these philanthropies, the variety of forms they take, and the degree to which they have succeeded in attracting support (especially from women with little previous history of involvement in

NEW DIRECTIONS FOR PHILANTHROPIC FUNDRAISING, NO. 2, WINTER 1993 © JOSSEY-BASS PUBLISHERS

philanthropy) hold lessons for everyone concerned with encouraging women's philanthropy.

What is a women's fund?

A women's fund is a philanthropy that focuses its grantmaking and other programs on issues that principally affect women and girls and that is governed and managed predominantly by women. The National Network of Women's Funds (NNWF), the membership organization that promotes and assists the development of women's funds and monitors the progress of women's philanthropy, reports that at the end of 1992, there were sixty-three such funds in some stage of development in the United States and Canada. While a few of these funds, such as the Ms. Foundation for Women, Women's Way in Philadelphia, the Astraea National Lesbian Action Foundation, and the Women's Foundation in San Francisco, have been operating since the 1970s, most of them have been in existence for less than ten years. From 1985, when NNWF was established, through the end of 1992, women's funds have distributed over $36 million in grants and allocations to a wide range of women's programs and projects, many of which had never received foundation support before.

For many years, nonprofit organizations have raised funds primarily from members of specific interest groups on behalf of the groups themselves. Perhaps the best known of these nonprofits are the United Negro College Fund and the United Jewish Appeal. Their existence is a commonsense matter of self-help and problem solving by those most directly affected by the issues the funds address. Women's funds are being organized with this same self-help emphasis: to develop and to focus the resources (human and financial) of women to address gender-specific needs. The funds offer women new ways of participating in decisions about how their money will be used. At the same time, the funds provide support to programs and projects that have been neglected by traditional philanthropy.

Reasons for growth

Women of wealth and privilege have always had a place, albeit often not an equal place, in the philanthropic sector. In some cases, they have directed their resources and influence to causes that supported the empowerment of other women, especially in the areas of education, women's suffrage, and advances in reproductive freedom. But for the most part, traditional philanthropies, as well as many women donors and volunteers, remained uninterested in—and in some cases, actively opposed to—investing in efforts centered on women's special needs. Skepticism about the importance of gender-specific programs still pervades the grantmaking and fundraising world, and it continues to be true that fewer than 5 percent of the total grant dollars awarded by traditional foundations and corporate giving programs are directed to programs designed specifically to serve women and girls. It is not coincidental that women are also underrepresented on the boards and at the top staff levels of these philanthropies. Women and Foundations/Corporate Philanthropy (WAF/CP), a national organization of grantmakers, has worked assiduously since the mid 1970s to focus attention on these disparities. At the same time, many who share WAF/CP's goals have also recognized the need for proactive efforts aimed at building alternative philanthropies directed to women's issues.

During the 1970s and 1980s, particularly, many women focused increased attention on a number of issues related to themselves and money, recognizing that they had more financial responsibilities and possibilities, more financial freedom, and even more desire to shape that freedom than women of preceding generations had displayed. With this recognition came a need for knowledge about financial matters and about the uses to which investments at every level are put. The concurrent entry of more and more women into the work force helped women learn to place a higher value than before on their volunteer time. Finally, many women, alerted by their own situations and the social changes happening all around them, focused more and more attention on the situation of all women (and of girls) and on the ways that issues that affect women first and hardest (employment insecurity, poverty, health care, child care, reproductive rights, domestic violence, sexual assault, educational inequities, and others) have an impact on all of society.

As women related these concerns to the role of women as donors and volunteers, a number of needs and beliefs emerged that led more or less directly to the growth of the women's funding movement. While every women's fund is organized and administered differently, each shares at least three characteristics: a desire to increase support and develop more reliable resources for woefully underfunded women's organizations and projects, a commitment to giving women a significant presence in the philanthropic community, and a belief in the importance of inclusiveness and self-determination—thus, a common goal of women's funds is to bring together people diverse in race, class, age, and experience. Women's funds actively recruit women of diverse economic levels and social backgrounds and work to encourage them to become active philanthropists.

Goals and structure

Women's funds present an interesting study for those who wish to tap the potential of women donors and volunteers. In part, this interest focuses on the funds' emphasis on donor inclusiveness and their success at engaging more women as donors. It would be regrettable, however, if the only lesson nonprofits learn from the women's funding movement is how to tailor giving opportunities to the psychology of women, because there is more to be learned. Much of the attraction of the women's funding movement for donors and volunteers has to do with the way the funds are structured, the way decisions are made within the funds, the variety of ways in which women can participate in the funds, and the causes to which the funds are applied.

Women's funds provide thousands of women with opportunities

that few but the most privileged women would find in most other philanthropic forums. These opportunities for women include having a voice in shaping the programmatic emphasis of their funds, participating in the grantmaking process through site visits and service on allocations committees, and contributing to decisions about the investment policies and the legal and administrative structure of the fund itself.

Among the first critical decisions made when a women's fund is established is the one about how future decisions will be made. Many women's funds are attempting to do away with traditional hierarchical decision-making methods, recognizing that, under these models, power and privilege tend to override the voices of diversity, even when there is nominal inclusiveness on the board roster. This attentiveness to living and working by the values espoused by their organizations has made governance a complicated and challenging, but also rewarding, experience for women in women's funds. It has also attracted many gifted women who have previously felt, and rightly so, that traditional philanthropy had no place for them. Long experience with exclusion and the conviction that true diversity will result in sounder grantmaking have led women's funds to recruit board members among women from many backgrounds. If their concerns about diversity are to result in more than superficial efforts, women's funds are forced to explore carefully such questions as whether they wish to mandate certain levels of participation (for example, the number of women of color or the number from different geographical areas) or set participative goals. If a fund elects to approach diverse representation through goal setting, it must then find ways to ensure that it adheres to the goals.

Another key organizational decision is when to begin grantmaking. Some funds have elected to wait until they have secured a certain level of resources; others have decided that it is important to begin as quickly as possible, both in order to build a fund's visibility and reputation and to get funding to grantees as quickly as possible. A related decision is whether to create an endowment or put as much as possible of the money raised into grants. Funds must also decide their grantmaking objectives: whether to provide general operating grants, special projects grants, or a combination of the two; whether to emphasize issues or focus on populations; and whether to establish grant initiatives or respond to community-based requests. Concurrently, funds must determine whether they prefer to make a few large grants or more small ones.

Funds must articulate their policies about critical issues, even if the policy is to have no position. Some funds undertake an advocacy role on certain issues that they believe to be at the core of the funds' values. Others believe that it is important to attract and serve women of the widest possible range of beliefs and therefore elect not to adopt an organizational position on certain issues. Related to policy decisions about critical issues are policy decisions about screening donors and/or declining support (or agreeing not to seek support) from funding sources (usually corporate or organizational) whose philosophies, products, or ways of operating conflict with the funds' values and with policies about the investment of the funds' assets.

Developing the answers to these questions and to others that range from the geographical scope of the funds to whether and how to offer donors such options as donor-designated and donor-advised funds has provided the women involved with women's funds the chance to experience true ownership of their own philanthropy. Women donors to women's funds who do not elect to participate as volunteers or trustees are often attracted to supporting the funds when they learn not only where their money is directed, but also how carefully—and inclusively—those decisions are made.

Women's funds are attempting to do several very difficult things simultaneously. They are identifying new donors (particularly women) and educating people of all income levels to become active philanthropists. They are working to diversify and democratize philanthropy by bringing new and previously unheard voices onto their own boards and grant/allocation committees. Women's funds are identifying new leaders within the funds' communities and offering a training ground for women to go on to other leadership positions within the public and private sectors. They are serving as a resource for traditional philanthropies about the concerns of women and girls and acting as a catalyst for discussion and change. The funds are introducing women's nonprofits, many of which are grassroots organizations with limited resources, to the wider world of philanthropic support. Finally, the funds are, in many cases, trying to develop and implement governance and management models that do not simply mirror traditional male-dominated hierarchical organizations. There is and probably always will be dispute among psychologists and other scholars about the degree to which women and men naturally differ in their preferred communication, leadership, and decision-making styles. What seems inarguable, however, is that with the freedom to choose, many women have sought to explore nontraditional governance and management models and have found the results rewarding.

Women's funds are truly "philanthropy in a different voice" as Marcia Shapiro Rose of Florida Atlantic University has called them (1992). Without question, this ongoing effort to encourage philanthropy by and for women is filled with challenges. Women's issues are still considered fringe issues by many in philanthropy and in society at large, and the women involved with the funds are often stereotyped or marginalized. Fundraising for women's issues and therefore for women's funds remains difficult. One woman, a prominent philanthropist and fundraiser in her community, who has also cochaired a major gifts campaign for a women's fund, reported that the women's fund campaign was the hardest fundraising she had ever done. She was struck by the different standards foundations, corporations, and even individuals used in evaluating requests from women's funds as opposed to their evaluations of requests from other organizations.

Individual women, of course, are the most logical constituency for women's funds and other women's programs. However, women, even those with resources, still often feel financially vulnerable and may, thus, be less willing or accustomed to give at the same level as men. Women are also less likely to have been educated when young about money and how to manage it. Some women with wealth have advisors managing their money and may not be involved in the decisions about how it is invested and spent. Some women do not share control of money equally with their spouses. Women's funds are not interested in simply separating women from their money to advance the funds' goals, however worthy. These funds are interested in encouraging women to understand and to use the power that they hold. Women's funds also consciously invest time and resources to attract support from women at levels that would be considered negligible by many other nonprofit organizations. This is an effort both to include donors from all economic backgrounds and to develop an understanding and a habit of considered giving among women unaccustomed to believing that their investments can matter.

Less than ten years old, most women's funds are underfinanced. They were created in response to a huge gap between the special needs of women and girls and the resources being provided to fill those needs. Community expectations of women's funds tend to be high, and women's funds are working to meet these expectations while also grappling with their own organization development issues. The internal and external pressures to get dollars to the community have sometimes meant that organizational capacity building has suffered, thus increasing the pressures even further. At the end of 1991, only thirty of the women's funds had begun to create endowments, for example, and many, though not all, of those endowments were relatively small (under $1 million). While women's funds are justifiably proud of their levels of accomplishment in a relatively short period of time, most also recognize that their organizational stability and growth are directly linked to the development of an expanded base of support. As the funds grow so too will their credibility and influence in the philanthropic community.

One of the most remarkable consequences of the women's funding movement is the genuine excitement it has sparked in women. In part, the excitement comes from women's passion for the issues involved. In part, it is related to having a chance to challenge the status quo, to call attention to overlooked and underfunded needs and concerns and to put financial leverage to work to meet those needs. And it also comes from women's being asked to move into a different league as donors and as fundraisers. For example, Carol Mollner describes one prominent Minneapolis lawyer, in the early stages of the development of the Minnesota Women's Fund, who remarked that she was, for the first time, really excited about fundraising. She went on to explain that she thought that women's organizations had historically set their sights too low; now, she said, there was an opportunity to move beyond the bake sale that was too often a fundraising mainstay. She, and other women, are excited about being asked to give—and get—large amounts on behalf of a cause that is vital to them.

With some notable exceptions, women have historically been relegated to the least powerful positions in organized philanthropy. This exclusion has harmed women, certainly, but those active in the women's funding movement believe that the resulting narrowed vision has also harmed philanthropies, whose broad social goals might be more effectively attained by adopting policies and practices that are genuinely inclusive.

It is worth considering whether the relatively low level of women's giving to a wide variety of causes is connected not only to women's perceived and real difference in capacity but also to their relative lack of interest because they and their concerns have been treated as unimportant. If this is the case, no amount of window dressing on the part of grant seekers will make much difference. Only a real and demonstrated commitment to inclusiveness and respect for all will capture the resources of women who are coming to value their own contributions more and more. The self-respect and self-help that the women's funding movement is fostering among women throughout the United States can enrich all of U.S. philanthropy in many ways, only one of which is financial.

Reference

Rose, M. S. "Philanthropy in a Different Voice." Paper prepared for the Department of Sociology and Social Psychology, Florida Atlantic University, and presented at the annual ARNOVA conference at Yale University, New Haven, Conn., 1992.

SUSAN CHURCH *is executive director of the Michigan Women's Foundation.*

CAROL MOLLNER *is executive director of the National Network of Women's Funds.*

Women's participation in the political process has evolved from their serving only as volunteers to their leveraging their financial philanthropy to influence the selection and election of candidates. Coordinated philanthropic efforts on behalf of women's political interests suggest a new avenue for women's power and influence.

9

Women, money, and political clout

Karen D. Stone, Susan F. Rice, Judith C. Angel

IN THE PAST, because donors have often not treated women political candidates seriously, it has been very difficult for these candidates to raise money. Women who attempted to run for elective office in the 1960s and 1970s watched as male politicians successfully tapped an affluent old boys' network of contributors. However, in recent years the tremendous fundraising edge that male candidates used to enjoy is being challenged. The overwhelming reason for this new fundraising success is that women are stepping up to fill the coffers of female candidates.

The year 1992 was the "year of the woman" not only because a record number of female candidates ran for and were elected to the U.S. House of Representatives and Senate but also because of the outpouring of campaign contributions from women supporting women. (For an overview of women's political action committees [PACs] see Baruch, 1993, p. 120.) In her 1992 California campaign for U.S. Senator, Barbara Boxer raised over $10 million, more

NEW DIRECTIONS FOR PHILANTHROPIC FUNDRAISING, NO. 2, WINTER 1993 © JOSSEY-BASS PUBLISHERS

money than *any* other senatorial candidate, male or female. More than two-thirds of the contributors were women. Lynn Yeakel, the Democratic nominee for senator in Pennsylvania, and a virtual political unknown, was perhaps the most direct beneficiary of the phenomenon of women supporting women. Women overwhelmingly funded Yeakel's unsuccessful challenge against incumbent senator and Senate Judiciary Committee member Arlen Specter. An analysis of the $1.7 million in total contributions received by Yeakel through July 15, 1992, showed that over 70 percent of the funds she raised were from out-of-state women; close to two-thirds of her contributions from Pennsylvanians were also from women. Beth Donovan noted that "without women donors, Yeakel would not be in the game" (1992, p. 3270). (Arlen Specter, winner of the race, was the recipient of $4.6 million, 82 percent of Specter's out-of-state money and 75 percent of his Pennsylvania money came from men.)

Women are agents of political change

For many years, women have actively participated in political campaigns. They have assumed a supportive role, answered telephones, stuffed envelopes, walked precincts. They have not written checks (see McCarthy, 1990). In many ways, the 1992 election was a watershed for women in the political process. The Senate Judiciary Committee's handling of Anita Hill's charges that U.S. Supreme Court nominee Clarence Thomas had sexually harassed her motivated women who had never before given to a political campaign to write checks to women candidates. In addition to the anger and awareness produced by the Thomas-Hill hearings, a belief that abortion rights were seriously threatened and a strengthened perception that women were seen as agents of change also motivated more women than ever before to contribute to women's political campaigns. "Women have learned that if they want to see themselves represented, they have to get behind women candidates with their contributions as well as their volunteer hours and their votes," says Ellen Malcolm, the creator of Emily's List (Donovan, 1992, p. 3270).

The phenomenal success of Emily's List itself (Emily is an acronym for Early Money Is Like Yeast—"it makes the dough rise") also illustrates the new financial power of women. In 1986, the year of its founding, Emily's List raised and directed $350,000 to women candidates it endorsed (pro-choice Democratic women); in 1990, $1.5 million was raised from 3,500 contributors. In 1992, Emily's List raised an extraordinary $6.2 million from over 24,000 donors, 90 percent of whom were women. This unusual group philanthropy was the biggest contributor to House and Senate candidates in the country. In 1992, Emily's List was, in effect, the largest PAC in the country.

Emerging influence of women

There are many lessons to be learned from women's unprecedented enthusiasm for female candidates, an enthusiasm that brought thousands of new female donors into the philanthropic system. The potential that women's fundraising among women can unlock for women, and for philanthropy in general, is staggering. A profound change in women's attitudes toward political giving has occurred and reflects women's emerging awareness of the potential of their new economic power for influencing politics. It further reflects women's willingness to use that economic power by the way they invest their money. Women are learning something men have traditionally understood: money provides access, and political giving is a smart investment.

Higher-earning working women

Harvard economists David E. Bloom and Sanders D. Korenman observe that "the growing economic clout of women is important to fundraisers because women—and especially single women—

allocate a larger share of their budgets to gifts, and make three times more cash contributions to charitable causes than men do" (Nichols, 1990, p. 87). Demographer Judith Nichols highlights some other significant demographic indicators about women that can influence women's new philanthropic posture (1990, p. 87):

• Women make up 53 percent of the work force.

• Women constitute 27 percent of business owners.

• Women are starting up new businesses at three times the rate of men.

• More women than men are graduating from college.

• Women are increasingly moving into the higher-paying professional and management careers.

• Many higher-earning women are single or married without children.

Given these demographic indicators, development professionals speculate that as women's earning power increases so will their ability to make sizable political and charitable gifts, both out of current income and through planned giving.

Nichols also writes that "women are becoming more assertive in supporting the organizations that interest them" (1990, p. 89). The significant increase in women's contributions to women candidates is a demonstration of this assertive behavior. "Women have a new awareness of the power of the dollars they control. Their attitudes toward choosing causes that reflect their personal interests and concerns have changed. Women who previously saw themselves as trustees for carrying on the support patterns of husbands and fathers, now see themselves as having a right to determine where the funds should go" (Nichols, 1990, p. 88). Clearly, the sheer number of women practicing political philanthropy and the combined impact of their gifts in influencing the successful election of women candidates is proof of a newly charged potential.

In order to better understand the significance of the recent tremendous increases in political giving of women, and to determine the implications for the nonprofit sector, development professionals will need to know more about the women who made these gifts. Evidence confirms that these new and increased contributions are coming from the higher-earning working women and more affluent nonworking women. However, as development professionals determine future fundraising strategies, they must realize that women are a diverse and complex market, and there is yet scant research about them.

Fundraising techniques of Emily's List and others

What can development professionals learn and apply from women's accelerated giving during the watershed political year of 1992? The phenomenon of women's increased giving—both in size of gifts and number of donors—has extraordinary implications for future fundraising successes. Standard fundraising techniques, such as involving volunteers and then asking them to donate, worked successfully in 1992. The increased urgency of the pro-choice issue, the threat of losing freedoms recently won, and the catalyst of the Thomas-Hill hearings resulted in an awareness and concern about a confluence of circumstances that made an effective case for fundraising, and the recognition of that case created unusual bonding and networking among women.

Create excitement

The most electrifying of the 1992 political fundraising efforts was the campaign by Emily's List. This PAC's 1992 campaign followed some basic development precepts. It had clearly defined goals, a sense of community, and value-driven excitement that appealed to the marketplace (see Thompson, 1992; Lord, 1983).

Target market segments

The purpose of Emily's List—to elect Democratic pro-choice women candidates—did indeed appeal to a large targetable market. Not only did the majority of the voters think the country would be governed better if more women held political office, but the majority of voters are women, and women are more inclined to vote and to vote pro-choice and Democratic (Pogrebin, 1990).

Another aspect of the market targeted by Emily's List was the appeal the PAC had for different segments of women. Both the younger working woman in the professional and managerial ranks and the older working woman play a significant role in this emerging market of potential donors. Today's older women are healthier and more affluent than ever before, they are more likely to retire with pension benefits, and (unlike nineteenth-century women) they will have complete control over their family's assets in the likely event that their husbands die before them. In addition, they are likely to spend more than the average householder on cash contributions (Braus, 1992).

Involve the volunteer

Furthermore, Emily's List created a powerful vehicle to receive funds. Although the donor channeled her contribution through Emily's List, she wrote the check directly to the campaign of the candidate she wanted to support. Thus, the donor was directly involved with the deposition of the gift. Such an opportunity for involvement in the use of the gift appears to be even more essential for women than for men donors (see Chapters Four and Five).

Emily's List used another important technique. It required donors to give a minimum gift of $100 to at least two pro-choice Democratic women candidates who had been assessed as potential winners in each election cycle. A donor could not be a member of Emily's List if she or he gave a smaller gift. This technique was valuable because setting this particular threshold for membership raised donors' gifts.

Be accountable

The 1992 Emily's List campaign made clear where the money was going and how it would be used, and the campaign also reported on the successes rung up by early money. Such reporting on the uses of funds satisfies another important criterion for successful fundraising accountability. The 1992 UCLA focus group findings also highlight the importance of this criterion for women donors (see Chapter Four).

Pay attention to the woman donor

From the increased involvement of women donors in the political process, we have derived thirteen recommendations for the development professional.

1. Pay careful attention to communicating a case that speaks to women's values.
2. Give women the credit they deserve. Record their gifts correctly (for example, do not credit husbands for wives' gifts).
3. Increase the representation of women on campaign committees and foundation boards.
4. Focus on the nuances of women as donors. For instance, women tend to ask more questions and desire more detail when being informed about gift-giving opportunities. Women who are donors also care as much as men donors about such fundraising criteria as positive thinking, truthfulness, honesty, and accountability (Payton, Rosso, and Tempel, 1991).
5. Involve women in gift-planning opportunities. Women enjoy the process of planning a gift and what it can do; however, be aware that donor cultivation takes longer when donors participate in planning (see Chapter Ten).
6. Create target projects that match the interests of specific women donors. These donors typically want to make a difference, and they want to empower others.
7. Publicize women's gifts. Emphasize how the use of women's gifts will impact and empower future generations. Women shy

away from publicity that suggests ego gratification, but once they understand that by publicizing individual gifts women can act as role models for other women, they may agree to publicity more often.

8. Create opportunities for women to apply their skills in an organization, to take ownership, and to provide leadership.

9. When preparing a fundraising campaign, apply the segmentation strategies suggested by Nichols (1990), but keep in mind that these approaches must be flexible and reevaluated often. For instance, working women in the managerial and professional ranks have more discretionary income than has been recognized and may be more receptive to a solicitation for a larger gift than is generally supposed. Many independently wealthy women want to be cultivated in their own right, not just as wives, daughters, or mothers.

10. Remember that the business of fundraising is philanthropy, not marketing. Women have a tradition of charitable giving and a desire to exercise philanthropic power and to empower others: "philanthropy lies at the heart of women's history" (McCarthy, 1990, p. x).

11. Establish stewardship programs, which continue to involve women in the results of their gifts.

12. Educate women on the power of philanthropy (Thompson, 1992).

13. Apply these concepts of fundraising to other activities: science and engineering programs for women, advocacy of social issues, support of women's foundations, and so on.

More women can give bigger donations

The potential for nonprofits to raise more money from women donors will escalate in the next decade. Historically, women have been philanthropic but have not felt encouraged to give as generously as they might have. The 1992 political campaign demonstrated to women that their money made a difference and truly affected change. Success is addictive. As women see the success of their money at work in elective politics and come to feel that they are a part of the political process, there is hope that they will continue to broaden and intensify their philanthropic involvement.

References

Baruch, L. D. (ed). "1992 Post-Election Wrap Up." *CAWP News and Notes*. Vol. 9, no. 1. New Brunswick, N.J.: Center for the American Woman and Politics, Eagleton Institute of Politics, Rutgers University, 1993.

Braus, P. "Women of a Certain Age." *American Demographics*, Dec. 1992, pp. 44–49.

Donovan, B. "Women's Campaigns Fueled Mostly by Women's Checks." *Congressional Quarterly*, Oct. 17, 1992, pp. 3269–3273.

Lord, J. G. *The Raising of Money*. Cleveland, Ohio: Third Sector Press, 1983.

McCarthy, K. D. (ed.). *Lady Bountiful Revisited: Women Philanthropy and Power*. New Brunswick, N.J.: Rutgers University Press, 1990.

Malcolm, E. *Notes from EMILY*, 1992, 7 (entire issue 5).

Nichols, J. *Changing Demographics: Fund-Raising in the 1990's*. Chicago: Bonus Books, 1990.

Payton, R. L., Rosso, H. A., and Tempel, E. R. "Taking Fund-Raising Seriously: An Agenda." In D. F. Burlingame and L. J. Hulse (eds.), *Taking Fund-Raising Seriously: Advancing the Profession and Practice of Raising Money*. San Francisco: Jossey-Bass, 1991.

Pogrebin, L. C. "Contributing to the Cause." *New York Times Sunday Magazine*, Apr. 22, 1990, pp. 22–24.

Stone, K., and Sublett, D. "The UCLA Women and Philanthropy Focus Groups Reports." Unpublished report. Office of Development, University of California, Los Angeles, 1992.

Thompson, A. I. "Women and Philanthropy." Unpublished preliminary report on the Wingspread conference "Women and Philanthropy," Racine, Wis., Oct. 1992.

KAREN D. STONE *is associate director of university development at UCLA and codirector of UCLA's Women and Philanthropy Program.*

SUSAN F. RICE *is president and CEO of the Greater Los Angeles Zoo Association and former president of the League of Women Voters of California.*

JUDITH C. ANGEL *is director of UCLA Professional Schools Development.*

By consciously approaching women through their own values and needs, Wellesley College's successfully completed capital campaign demystified and debunked the notion that women's philanthropy is limited.

10

Raising money for women from women: The story of a successful campaign

Nicki Newman Tanner, Peter Ramsey

IN APRIL 1992, Wellesley College announced the successful completion of a campaign for $150 million, a five-and-one-half-year capital campaign that eventually raised $168 million in gifts and pledges. In addition, the college received $173 million in gifts in-kind of art, books, and equipment. Although Wellesley thus broke all fundraising records for liberal arts colleges, this would not, ordinarily, be the stuff of news releases. What made the campaign newsworthy was the gender of the record breakers. Not only were three of the first four liberal arts colleges to raise over $100 million in specific campaign efforts women's colleges (Smith, Wellesley, Pomona, and Mt. Holyoke), but two women's colleges (Wellesley and Smith) ranked numbers one and two in total private gift support each year during their campaign years compared to *all* liberal arts colleges. Furthermore, when compared to all liberal arts colleges and universities during the campaign year 1989–90, Welles-

NEW DIRECTIONS FOR PHILANTHROPIC FUNDRAISING, NO. 2, WINTER 1993 © JOSSEY-BASS PUBLISHERS

ley raised the highest average per capita dollar gift (total alumnae giving divided by alumnae solicited).

The stories and articles that appeared in magazines and newspapers around the country made note of this phenomenon with varying degrees of incredulity, and some development professionals began to ask questions: *Why* do alumnae of women's colleges give more to their alma maters than alumnae of coed schools or, indeed, than all alumni of coed schools? In what sense were campaigns at women's colleges different from those at other institutions? Did women's colleges do anything that others might learn from and use successfully? We will try to address these questions, based on our institution's campaign experience, but first it is important to provide some background about Wellesley and its particular culture.

The Wellesley College culture

The college was founded in 1870 by Henry Fowle Durant, an unusual man whose radical attitudes and independent zeal inform the college's mission today. In 1875, Mr. Durant declared in a sermon: "The Higher Education of Women is one of the great world battle cries for freedom, for right against might. . . . I believe that God's hand is in it; that it is one of the great ocean currents of Christian civilization; that He is calling to womanhood to come up higher, to prepare herself for great conflicts, for vast reforms in social life, for noblest usefulness." Although much has changed in the world, education, and the lives of women since Wellesley's founding, Durant's vision of a college committed to preparing women for lives of leadership and service endures, and his phrase "for noblest usefulness" can be heard on Wellesley's campus today in song and sermon and read in the college's current recruitment and fundraising brochures.

From the beginning, Wellesley College was unusual in the opportunities it provided for women to take leadership positions. Wellesley's first president, Ada L. Howard, was the first woman college president in the world, and throughout its 118-year history, Wellesley is the one major college to have had *only* women presidents and one of a small handful whose faculty has at least half of its tenured positions filled by women.

Shared governance has also been important in the Wellesley culture from the college's earliest days to the present, and the 1990 reaccreditation team representing the Commission on Institutions of Higher Education of the New England Association of Schools and Colleges singled out "the intense and unusually active involvement of the faculty and students in the governance of the college" as one of Wellesley's "unique characteristics." This unusually active involvement extends to Wellesley alumnae, trustees, administration, and staff as well—constituencies that place a high value on partnerships and collaborative enterprises.

Careful planning has been another of Wellesley's hallmarks, and a 1984–85 strategic planning process preceded our capital campaign by a year and provided many of the arguments for the case for the campaign.

All these features, namely, a culture of support for women, a tradition of shared governance, alumnae support, and careful planning, along with a strong academic reputation and a healthy endowment, should have justified cautious optimism. But the needs identified by our 1984 Plans and Priorities Committee and the committee's conclusion that at least $125 million was required to address those needs made us ask how much the college could reasonably expect to raise.

Planning for fundraising from alumnae

Campaign counsel suggested four basic requirements for a goal in the range of $125 to $150 million:

1. One or two gifts at the level of $5 million or more.
2. A minimum of $70 million to come from the top 90 to 100 gifts.

3. The majority of giving to come from individuals, principally alumnae, since Wellesley was not a research university that could command extraordinary support from corporations and foundations.
4. Existing yearly giving in the range of $14 million to $15 million would have to double to $30 million in three to four years.

These requirements were sobering. While Wellesley had always enjoyed considerable success in fundraising (raising $72 million in nine years during a centennial campaign in the 1970s) and annually averaged around 53 to 54 percent in alumnae participation, the college's two previous largest gifts had been in the range of $2.5 million. In general, the nation's liberal arts colleges were still finding it difficult to secure gifts at the $1 million level, and this pattern was especially true among the women's colleges.

We also had concerns that had to do with society's perceptions of women and women's perceptions of themselves. It was assumed by many development professionals that raising money from women for a women's institution offered particular challenges, owing to women's supposed fear of, discomfort with, or disinterest in money. There was a sense that many women considered it "unladylike" to talk about money, that dollars put up barriers that interfered with the egalitarian nature of "sisterhood." Other development professionals hastened to add that women did not like to fundraise: they considered charitable work a substitute for giving, and when they *did* give, their idea of a leadership gift was pitifully small. "Everyone knew" that most women felt that men were entitled to give more to their schools because they earned more money or because their schools enabled them to earn more money, that women's issues were marginal to mainstream concerns, and— the coup de grace—that since women today had "made it," women's education was no longer necessary, but was a contemporary dinosaur, on its way to extinction.

Awareness of these attitudes furrowed the brow, to say the least.

Wellesley's campaign leadership recognized that to reach the ambitious goal of $150 million, it had three major tasks: first, to mount a major outreach effort to sustain and build confidence in the institution, its continuing importance for women, and its academic strength and financial health; second, to challenge, directly and indirectly, the above-mentioned perceptions about women donors; and third, to involve as many people as possible in the fundraising process.

Inclusivity and involvement

Before the campaign's official starting date, Wellesley began substantive outreach efforts. The first was a series of twenty-five Dialogue Dinners held in seventeen cities around the country, attended by alumnae donor prospects and the husbands of the married alumnae. Before each dinner, attendees received the college president's paper on her vision for the college, and this vision served to frame the dinner discussions. Afterward, each attendee (and each spouse) was given a questionnaire and asked to respond to the president's paper and the discussion and to indicate her or his relative interest in the various proposed needs. These dinners were important on many levels. First, they provided, together with the report of the Plans and Priorities Committee, the framework for the case for the campaign. Second, they offered several hundred of our most important donor prospects an opportunity to become informed, informing (in relation to others), and involved. They reminded alumnae, in a convivial setting, of the continuing excellence and strength of Wellesley and encouraged them to think about their relationship to and responsibility for its future.

Another important outreach effort was the building of what fundraisers call a nucleus fund, namely, that amount of money raised before a campaign goes public. Raising this early money requires an institution to hone its arguments and carefully listen to the responses of the earliest donor prospects. Because the board of trustees is in the best position to understand and, by their support, validate the goals of a campaign, its members are critical to this focusing process. Fortunately for Wellesley, many members of its board made an early and strong commitment to the campaign, and a $5 million gift from trustee Kathryn Wasserman Davis gave a hefty boost to the nucleus fund total while making a powerful statement about women and philanthropy. By the end of the campaign, not only had two-thirds of the board members either chaired or cochaired regional campaigns in their area of the country, but the board also could boast of 100 percent participation among its thirty-six members, accounting for $20 million, or 12 percent of the total finally raised.

The printed materials—the most visible aspect of any campaign—were designed to build confidence in the enterprise. Campaign brochures, titled variously "The Economics of Excellence," "Ever New, Ever Wellesley," and "Investing in Leadership," were handsome and informative, carefully outlining and justifying the needs of the college relative to the goals of the campaign. Outside columns down the large pages of the campaign newsletter, *Work in Progress*, were devoted to the voices of the volunteer leadership. There was a conscious effort to emphasize, in every way possible, the inclusivity of the campaign and the diversity of those who were involved as donors and volunteers.

Kickoffs were held in forty-seven geographical regions over the two and one-half years of the campaign's public phase. Wellesley invited *all* alumnae to a kickoff as guests of the college. This decision was an expensive one, and many campaigns do it differently, inviting only those from whom they can reasonably expect a contribution and/or charging for the event. For Wellesley, inviting everyone was the right decision, as the celebrations turned out to be important confidence builders and consciousness raisers. On the one hand, there was a conscious effort to make the kickoffs stylistically comparable to fundraising events of male-dominated institutions. They were elegant and festive; they conveyed self-assurance and strength. On the other hand, in substance, they were typical of Wellesley in that the messages articulated by the campaign leaders were always personal ones, written by them and reflecting the leaders' own responses to the various needs put forward by the college.

Educating volunteers and staff

Given prevailing attitudes about women and fundraising, it was important for us to work to build confident fundraisers. Silent screening sessions were designed to counter alumnae's past reluctance to discuss others' financial capabilities. Alumnae were asked to look at a prospect list and suggest—on paper and only for the women they knew—a gift range and area(s) of possible philanthropic interest. Volunteer fundraisers were assured that the most important object of their personal calls on potential donors was to make a connection between each alumna and her college; therefore their personal calls could not fail. They were reminded that women across the country were finding work as professional development officers congenial to their talents and temperaments and that women tended to possess some of the most important characteristics of good fundraisers: graciousness, sensitivity, and strong listening skills. They were encouraged to role-play solicitation visits, including the discussion before the call, the call itself, the "ask," and the response.

The purposes of the printed material, the nucleus fund, and the regional kickoffs were to reach out and to inspire confidence. The campaign oratory was designed to raise consciousness and challenge preconceptions. We used every meeting, from the smallest fundraising workshop to the largest gathering, as an opportunity to confront preconceptions about women and philanthropy and question whether or not they applied to the women in the meeting. The women, both staff and alumnae, attending the meetings made each other allies in the challenge, analyzing each other in relation to their Wellesley experiences and to available data. Each time perception and reality were found to be at odds, we went public with our findings.

The newspaper article "Alma Maters Court Their Daughters" (Matthews, 1991) provided much grist for this particular mill and gave us excellent opportunities to extol the virtues of a women's college and to demonstrate its ongoing value in today's society. The article claimed that "women's donations to higher education [were] lackluster" and described three categories of women: those who outlive their husbands and donate only to the husband's college, in his name, for projects he would have approved; those who do not make financial decisions beyond household budgets; and those who argue that "it's my money and I deserve to keep it" (p. 42). Whenever possible during the campaign, we referred to and refuted the claims of this article, saying that, since our total gifts to date were anything but lackluster, was it not reasonable to assume that graduates of women's colleges were atypical and did not fit the author's thesis? This argument also allowed us to segue logically to a reminder that a women's college, compared to other colleges, was still the *one* institution of higher education where women participated fully in campus life in and out of class. In addition, women educated at women's colleges majored more often in nontraditional fields for women, such as math and physics; were more than three times as likely to go on to medical school; went on to earn more doctorates; and had and held on to higher levels of self-esteem than women educated at other institutions. Then, sensing a positive response from the alumnae, we took our argument one bold step forward, saying, "A place like Wellesley has a special value as a model. If, for some, Wellesley is seen as atypical, then we have a responsibility to correct that—since if Wellesley were *typical* in its encouragement of women to take initiative and to take risks, without limitations, fear, or constraints, the world would be a better place."

This kind of talk, direct, confident and a mite assertive, does not come trippingly to women's tongues. But the more we spoke out, the more exciting it became to suggest publicly that the world would benefit from what intelligent, well-educated, and confident women could bring to it. It was thrilling to approach each alumna as an adult, capable of understanding the issues about women as donors underlying our campaign and of making responsible choices among those issues. And it was *fun* to raise questions and then shoot them down. Nice women do not like to talk about money? Nonsense! Women consider volunteer efforts their contribution? No longer! Women's concerns are outside the mainstream? In today's political climate, we argued, being on the outside—what someone in our campaign called "a flash of fuchsia in a sea of gray"—having concern for the young, the aged, the sick, and the environment might well be the preferred place to be.

To those who were married, we urged parity in giving and joint decision making about how the couple's philanthropic dollar was to be spent. We challenged the notion that husbands were entitled to give more to their schools, arguing that women's roles in society were equally important, whether they were providing leadership in classrooms, soup kitchens, or corporate boardrooms.

Campaign results

Meanwhile, the number of bold gifts to our campaign, many of them first-time contributions, was growing, and we were meeting the four basic requirements suggested by counsel at the beginning of the campaign. We did receive a gift of $5 million and a gift of $10 million, and a total of $73 million from the top sixty-four gifts, but the majority of giving did come from individuals, who contributed $147 million (88 percent of the total), with $133 million (79 percent of the total) coming from alumnae (see Tables 10.1 and 10.2). The average yearly giving of $14 million to $15 million in fiscal years 1983, 1984, and 1985 did double—to $28 million in 1989 and 1990 and $32 million in 1991 and in 1992.

Of course, every significant donor was gratefully and affectionately recognized in all the campaign publications and at every other

Table 10.1. Gifts by Dollar Amount

Range	Number of Donors	Total Value
$5,000,000+	2	$16,587,000
2,500,000–4,999,999	2	5,535,000
1,000,000–2,499,999	23	29,039,000
500,000–999,999	37	23,524,000
250,000–499,999	62	20,663,000
100,000–249,999	135	18,141,000
50,000–99,999	168	10,871,000
25,000–49,999	353	11,029,000
10,000–24,999	835	11,815,000
5,000–9,999	1,158	7,129,000
1,000–4,999	4,230	8,708,000
Up to 999	23,398	4,986,000
Total	**30,403**	**$168,027,000**

opportunity. A leadership gift ($100,000 and up) committee had been formed early, with sixty women as members, each with the joint responsibilities of giving at the leadership level herself and of approaching alumnae who had been identified as having leadership gift potential.

The Wellesley campaign put women's concerns unabashedly front and center, emphasizing the importance of women's edu-

Table 10.2. Gifts by Source

Sources	Total Value
Alumnae	$133,802,000
Parent, husbands, and friends	13,309,000
Clubs	1,031,000
Corporations	0
Grants	1,952,000
Matching gifts	4,028,000
Foundations	13,905,000
Total	**$168,027,000**

cation as an investment in future leaders for all areas of human endeavor and social concern. Alumnae were reminded—continuously—of the common goals and shared values that they cherished, particularly the value of a liberal arts education and of a community that takes women seriously. The result surprised even the most confident among us. As can be seen in Tables 10.1 and 10.2, while enormously successful at the leadership gift level, the effort was also broad based and inclusive, with an astonishing *81 percent* of all alumnae solicited during the period of the campaign making one or more gifts.

Lessons learned

From an organizational point of view, several factors stand out as integral to the campaign's success. Because Wellesley does not have an annual fund drive, alumnae were not subjected to what is often referred to as the double ask. Rather, they were asked to make the largest yearly gift they could for whatever purpose(s) they perceived as most important to them and to their alma mater. An open gift-crediting policy, whereby both outright and irrevocable deferred gifts (the latter accounted for approximately $16 million) were given equal credit, supported the asking process and enabled volunteers to work freely with their prospects.

Among the many important lessons we learned during the course of the campaign was the advantage of a flexible, evolving fundraising structure that permitted quick changes when new concerns or ideas emerged from volunteer leaders or alumnae prospects in the field. Take, for example, the case of our proposal letters. During the earliest regional campaigns, volunteers from one region thought the two-page proposal letter designed by development staff to support personal solicitation visits for gifts in the $5,000 to $25,000 range was too short, so the staff wrote a longer one, with positive results. Meanwhile, volunteers in another region were arguing for a single-page proposal letter. The staff obliged again, with positive results there as well. This kind of flexibility, which we found so important, is, we have been told, atypical of fundraising drives.

We also learned the merits of inclusivity. The decision to invite all alumnae, regardless of giving potential, to the regional kickoff celebrations and to send all alumnae the same quality of campaign materials pitted inclusivity's merits against its costs. Table 10.3, a comparison of randomly selected donors' campaign commitments and their largest previous gifts, stands as a warning against development officers' prejudging donor prospects and indicates the wisdom of opting for inclusivity.

We learned to prize support staff with an esprit de corps to carry them through the occasional stressful moments and (perceived) twenty-eight hour days, and the good humor and flexibility to work

Table 10.3. Campaign Commitments and Previous Gifts from Randomly Selected Donors

Campaign Commitment	Largest Previous Gift
$1,001,000	$100,000
770,000	5,000
753,000	150,000
607,000	5,000
527,000	150,000
500,000	3,500
500,000	0
500,000	500
451,000	5,000
350,000	250
302,000	25,000
287,000	58,000
267,000	75
260,000	5,000
260,000	500
250,000	0

with a diverse alumnae population. We gained an even greater appreciation of the volunteer-staff partnership and the value of a decision-making process that involved 2,500 volunteers and a 52-person development staff. Yes, it was time consuming. Yes, it was labor intensive. But it gave everyone a sense of ownership that ultimately stood the campaign in good stead.

We discovered the silver lining to the women-don't-like-to-pledge cloud. While it was true that alumnae discomfort with debt meant that only half of the alumnae donors were willing to pledge over a three- to five-year period (a circumstance that created more work for volunteers and staff over the course of the campaign), we now suspect that our consequent need to return annually to a number of donor prospects may have provided the long-term benefit of strengthened connections between those alumnae and the college. There was also a short-term benefit to alumnae debt discomfort and that benefit is quantifiable: because many alumnae chose to fulfill their commitments early, a *91 percent* fulfillment rate by the last day of the campaign meant that Wellesley had a whopping $153 million already in its coffers on that day.

We learned not to shy away from asking students to help in fundraising. A campus-based student phoning program raised more than $2 million during the final two years of the public phase of the campaign and provided invaluable opportunities for connection—of students to the needs of their college and of students to alumnae. Students were also used, to great effect, in the post-campaign "thank-a-thon."

We learned that money thoughtfully spent can be an excellent investment. Despite the expensive kickoffs, campaign materials, and end-of-campaign celebrations, Wellesley spent only nine cents for every dollar raised.

We learned the advantage of having a campaign that is the priority of the institution's leadership. Wellesley owes a great debt to

• A tireless president who spoke at each of the forty-seven regional kickoffs and made over 350 personal visits.

- A board chair, three trustee national cochairs, and a campaign executive committee who respected one another and worked well together.

- A board and executive committee that considered the campaign worthy of being a major agenda item for every meeting.

- Alumnae who filled approximately 8,500 volunteer positions—2,500 of these volunteers were directly involved with fundraising and another 6,000 indirectly supported the fundraising effort by working in admissions, recruiting, class, club, and regional programs; career center services; and other activities.

Perhaps the most important lesson of all that we learned is the importance of this premise: *a fundraising campaign represents a window of time in the history of an institution, and it is incumbent upon the campaign leaders and professional staff to approach every potential prospect with a sensitivity to her or his individual position and lifelong relationship with the institution and its cause.* We are convinced that there is a danger of losing prospective donors when they are approached without the benefit of a strong institutional relationship; we are persuaded that donors who are unable to give or to commit during that window of time opened by the campaign can nonetheless become the foundation stones upon which subsequent campaigns will be built. These donors should not be devalued or forgotten.

In conclusion, we argue that it was the distinctly female character of Wellesley's capital campaign (and Smith's and Mt. Holyoke's) that accounted, to a large extent, for its success. Thanks to the work of researchers and writers Carol Gilligan (1982), Blythe Clinchy (1986), Deborah Tannen (1990), and others, development professionals have learned that women tend to experience the self as connected and that they espouse a morality based on care. Armed with that understanding, we offered Wellesley alumnae as many opportunities as possible to learn about and to connect with each other and with the college. We listened to them. We took their responses, suggestions, questions, and concerns seriously. We valued them. And because such attentiveness is still a rare experience for women in our society, the alumnae said thank you with great generosity.

While men and women do give for some of the same reasons, there are strong motivational factors that are particular to women. In 1988, a questionnaire on women and charitable giving was filled out anonymously by 137 women attending the annual meeting of Wellesley's Alumnae Leadership Council. The questionnaire produced two findings of particular interest: first, Wellesley was the most commonly cited influence on alumnae attitudes toward philanthropic giving (cited more frequently than parents, religion, or spouse), and second, 95 percent of the respondents believed women had a particular responsibility to support women's institutions. The sample was small and selective, but there were many echoes of these sentiments during our campaign. This recurring theme of felt responsibility is quite different from fundraising approaches that address feelings of peer pressure or competition: for example, "Bill X and Bob Z have agreed to contribute $10,000. I know you've had a good year, and you should be in their category." We have yet to meet the woman who would respond positively to that argument. Women who feel themselves to be in partnership with an institution and its enterprises will listen to a carefully presented proposal, and—if they share the values of the organization, if its needs match their interests, and if they have been included in the process, listened to, and taken seriously—they will give generously.

It will be interesting to see the extent to which Wellesley's modus operandi will serve as model for other institutions. To date, few institutions have modified their fundraising approaches to accommodate the women in their midst. University campaigns have been designed by men to raise money from men. But times change. Now that women make up half the undergraduate universe, as well as half of the graduating classes of MBA programs and law and medical schools, institutions that ignore their women are not only fiscally irresponsible but also shortsighted since women's perspectives and values can only enhance the fundraising environment.

Other women's voices have been reinforcing this theme of women's competence. Texas Governor Ann Richards, for example, made this wonderful observation at the 1992 Democratic National Convention: "Ginger Rogers did everything that Fred Astaire did. She just did it backwards and in high heels." To which *New York Times* writer Anna Quindlen later added, "Dancing backwards, in high heels, you may not learn the same steps that the boys learn. Then again, you know some moves that they will never know" (Quindlen, 1993, p. C14).

While it makes sense for fundraisers to look seriously at women's potential for philanthropic giving, it is also important that women learn to take their own philanthropic giving seriously. If more women participated actively and generously, fundraising would occur in a larger and different context. A fundraising approach based on Carol Gilligan's "web of concerns" (1982, p. 2), on relationships and responsibilities, would join the now favored, if limited, do-it-for-the-team approach. Women would thus participate in an important process of behavioral change, and as Wellesley professor of sociology Rosanna Hertz says, "If behaviors are changed, attitudes congruent with the change will often follow" (Rosanna Hertz, personal communication, 1992).

Women are learning that money can be a powerful tool. By becoming serious philanthropists, women can influence policies and behavior in public and private sectors just as men have always done. As feminist and philanthropist Sallie Bingham writes, "Wealthy men have always influenced the course of this nation's history. What a difference it would make to women as a whole if we became visible—actively involved in working out our own destiny" (1986, p. 82).

From our perspective, working with and raising money from women was a special opportunity, challenging and gratifying. We found that our willingness to speak, as Gilligan (1982) says, "in a different voice," listen athletically, and dance in somewhat different steps, led us to a gratifying and record-breaking success.

References

Belenky, M. F., Clinchy, B., and others. *Women's Ways of Knowing: The Development of Self, Voice, and Mind.* New York: Basic Books, 1986.

Bingham, S. *Ms. Magazine,* June 1986, p. 82.

Gilligan, C. *In a Different Voice.* Cambridge, Mass.: Harvard University Press, 1982.

Matthews, A. "Alma Maters Court Their Daughters." *New York Times Sunday Magazine,* Apr. 7, 1991, pp. 40–42.

Quindlen, A. *New York Times,* Nov. 21, 1993, p. C14.

Tannen, D. *You Just Don't Understand.* New York: Ballantine Books, 1990.

NICKI NEWMAN TANNER *is director of UJA–Federation of Jewish Philanthropies of New York Oral History Project. She was cochair of the Wellesley College campaign for $150 million and is currently chair of Wellesley's National Development and Outreach Council.*

PETER RAMSEY *is vice president for resources and public affairs at Wellesley College.*

Ethnic, religious, and sexual diversity highlights the complex nature of women's philanthropy today.

11

Richness in diversity

Susan Weidman Schneider, Gretchen von Schlegell

WHILE THERE IS GROWING RECOGNITION of women in general as philanthropists, fewer data exist on the philanthropic motivations of various ethnic, religious, and special-interest groups.

Donors of color

"Donors of Color" is the subject of a 1992 study by the Winters Group of Rochester, New York. The study considered African Americans, Asian Americans, and Hispanics. It was designed to help community foundations and other structured philanthropies reach out to these potential donors.

History and cultural traditions influence the philanthropic approaches of different ethnic groups. For example, part of the concept of philanthropy for some ethnic groups are "in-kind services" and nonstructured giving. African American participants agreed on the importance of supporting the church and noted it as the primary beneficiary of their charitable giving. Hispanics also included the church but cited as high priorities their immediate families and assisting causes in their native countries. Asian American respondents were likely to support their families and causes that

NEW DIRECTIONS FOR PHILANTHROPIC FUNDRAISING, NO. 2, WINTER 1993 © JOSSEY-BASS PUBLISHERS

directly support the Asian community. Some Asian Americans noted that charitable giving was not a concept from their own cultural background but rather one learned in the United States.

African American and Hispanic respondents indicated that their giving was directed by desires to give back to their community or to a cause that had benefitted them personally. Asian and Hispanic respondents were motivated also by public recognition.

We can infer from the findings of studies on why women give that traditional charities do not necessarily address the needs or agendas of African Americans, Hispanics, and Asian Americans. Interestingly, there is no research on the giving patterns of women within these three racial/ethnic groups.

Progressives

Philanthropies addressing the needs of lesbians and progressive women appeal to donors identified with these communities. The Astraea Foundation, the National Lesbian Action Foundation, was formed in 1977 by a group of women who were aware that many projects face funding difficulties because of their progressive and feminist perspectives. After making their first grant in 1980, these women established a fund to raise money for women's organizations and individuals concerned with issues such as economic disparity, multiculturalism, sexism, reproductive rights, and oppression faced by women and girls. Astraea raises and distributes funds. Through a program called Lesbian Visibility in Action, Astraea provides leadership development training and technical assistance, and sponsors an annual Lesbian Writers Fund.

Catholic tradition

Research specific to the religious interests of donors has been conducted by Sister Mary Oates of Regis College in Weston, Massachusetts (see *Faith and Good Works: The Catholic Philanthropic Tradition in America*, forthcoming).

The substantial charitable work in schools, hospitals, and orphanages of both religious and lay women has been largely overlooked in writings about Catholic charities over the past two hundred years. In addition, Catholics have been generally regarded as poor people with little to give, although Oates found many women "quite creative" in encouraging even the poorest to contribute. She suggests that the decline in Catholic giving over the past thirty years may be linked to the lack of "hands-on charity involvement" in large bureaucratic Catholic charities today (personal communication, Jan. 19, 1994).

Jewish women's philanthropy in the nineties

Open-ended interviews with more than one hundred women donors to Jewish causes formed the basis for two articles (Schneider, 1993a,b).

Jewish women are a bellwether for women's giving, for several reasons. First, they are the best-educated women in America today (64 percent of those between twenty-five and forty-five have college degrees, compared to about 18 percent of other white American women); their patterns of giving may indicate trends among female college graduates in general.

Second, Judaism emphasizes philanthropy, both to Jewish causes and to the general "repair" of the world. Also, family traditions of giving charity mean that even nonreligious Jews may find philanthropy a way to identify Jewishly. Especially for women, who were traditionally excluded from most public Jewish ritual, communal and charitable activities became alternative routes to participation and empowerment in the Jewish community.

Do Jewish women give differently from Jewish men or other women? Does the successful male fundraising method—peer pressure—boomerang for Jewish women (94 percent of women in a nationwide survey said they would give more to Jewish charities "if they were solicited differently")? How can Jewish women use their philanthropy to foster leadership opportunities for women in heretofore male-dominated Jewish religious and communal institutions?

The interviews suggest that men often characterize their giving to Jewish causes as obligatory and routine. Men tend to write the check first and *then* get asked to come to events or serve on a committee. Women's giving is more likely to come out of an understanding of the cause itself. "Men give to preserve institutions; women give to create new programs," reported one woman.

Fundraisers assume that a man will automatically want to give more money than a friend or business associate did. In contrast, most of the women interviewed did *not* want to outdo one another, considered intrusive the suggestion that they give a certain amount, and cared a great deal about where, specifically, their money was going.

Women donors may ask more questions than men do. One woman who was approached to help fund an athletic facility wanted to know, "Will women have equal access? Will there be facilities for the handicapped? Is a gym necessary, or is job training more urgent?" This concern for detail can be a strength in philanthropy. Women hold organizations more accountable," claimed one donor.

Men stress that "who asks" is important, but women establish commonality between solicitor and donor quickly in a shared laugh over a politician's gaffe or a sigh of understanding over child-rearing or workplace situations. The model of women talking in a group about their charitable giving, now being widely explored by fundraisers, is characteristic of Jewish women's charities.

The downside of the group situation is that a woman often tailors her giving to the level of those around her. This modesty carries a twofold liability. First, in contrast to men's giving, women may gives less than they can because they do not want to appear wealthier than their friends. Second, when women make large contributions anonymously, they cannot serve as role models for other women.

Jewish women may be particularly uneasy about being visible as donors. Historically, anti-Semitism has linked Jews and money. Jewish women have been victims of this bigotry in the form of "Jewish-American Princess" jokes, with their pernicious amalgam of anti-Semitism and misogyny.

Attitudes about money are also determined by the money's source: inherited, earned, or spousal. Women born into wealth often feel this money is not their own. ("How can I be an activist and also 'out' as a woman of wealth?" asked one.) Women who earn the money they give away are often elated to be donors.

Most married Jewish women interviewed make independent financial decisions *and* influence their husbands' giving. Women get credit only for the money they give in their own names (about 20 percent of the funds raised by Jewish charities), when they are in fact responsible for a much higher proportion of the total.

What about power? Women say they like to contribute to a range of organizations. By supporting fewer charities but giving more to each, women donors could wield greater influence. This practice would hurt the smaller, innovative charities that many women now support, charities that spawn new ideas, which later enter the mainstream. To maximize the influence of relatively small checks and encourage new projects, some women across the United States and Canada are creating Jewish women's funds.

What else does the future hold? Here are ten steps into the future of Jewish women's philanthropy that will help shape a richer future for all philanthropies involving women.

1. *Focus on the future.* Women live seven years longer than men, on average, and thus control a great deal of inherited wealth. Philanthropies had better stop being scornful of older women.

2. *Showcase women's issues.* Increasingly, women donors want to know that their support helps women. Only 5 percent of

foundation grants in the United States go to projects for girls and women. Women's issues can turn passive members into active donors. A feminist philanthropy is emerging, and Jewish women are interested in projects with both a Jewish and a women's component.

3. *Notice small changes.* Women are encouraging small-scale and grassroots giving when they ask that, in lieu of gifts for religious milestones or birthdays, food and toiletries be contributed to a battered women's shelter or books on women's subjects be given to a library.

4. *Watch the time line.* Women in North America are marrying and having their children later than their own mothers did. Volunteering—a precursor to becoming a donor for many women—also happens later for this generation. To attract women earlier, showcase projects with a visible feminist component.

5. *Draw in single women.* They may have significant disposable earned income and no dependents, yet single women are often ignored by a couples-oriented culture.

6. *Realize that women donors and participants are one.* Address the personal needs of women from whom you are soliciting money. People give to what they themselves experience or use.

7. *Appreciate diversity.* Emphasize programs important to different target populations. Women's interests shift according to age, level of education, sexual orientation, and ethnic or religious group.

8. *Train your daughters.* Talk to your daughters about what you support and why, and involve younger friends or relatives in establishing philanthropic priorities.

9. *Pump up the amounts women give.* Showcase women donors who make significant contributions. Establish opportunities for women to give—comfortably—more than they believed they could.

10. *Understand that women want a vote with their checks.* Donors can change an organization's priorities by asking, "What percentage of your board are women? What services directly benefit girls and women?" Prospective donors now say, "Come back to me once you have more women on your board. I'd consider making a contribution then." If organizations do not respond, savvy donors will take their checks elsewhere.

References

Schneider, S. W. "Women Funding Social Change." *LILITH*, Fall 1993a.
Schneider, S. W. "Jewish Women's Philanthropy." *LILITH*, Winter 1993b.
Winters Group. "Donors of Color." Unpublished report. Rochester, N.Y.: Winters Group and the Council on Foundations, 1992.

SUSAN WEIDMAN SCHNEIDER *is editor-in-chief of* LILITH, The Independent Jewish Women's Magazine. *The author of* LILITH's *series on philanthropy, she lectures widely and consults with community organizations on women's issues. She is the author of several books.*

GRETCHEN VON SCHLEGELL *is the daughter of this issue's coeditor Abbie von Schlegell. She is a senior at St. Lawrence University and is majoring in English and writing.*

12

Selected bibliography

Ann Castle

Books and reports

Addams, J. *Forty Years at Hull-House, with Autobiographical Notes*. New York: Macmillan, 1935.

Addis, P. K. *Through a Woman's I: An Annotated Bibliography of American Women's Autobiographical Writings 1946–1976*. Metuchen, N.J.: Scarecrow Press, 1983.

Alumnae Giving at Women's Colleges: A Ten-Year Report. Washington, D.C.: Women's College Coalition, 1988.

Astor, B. *Footprints*. New York: Doubleday, 1980.

Babcock, E. *Final Report: The Forum on Women in Philanthropy*. Indianapolis: Indiana University Center on Philanthropy, Apr. 1992.

Bonaviglia, A. *Far from Done: The Status of Women and Girls in America*. New York: Women and Foundations/Corporate Philanthropy, 1989.

Bonaviglia, A. *Making a Difference: The Impact of Women in Philanthropy*. New York: Women and Foundations/Corporate Philanthropy, 1991.

Bonaviglia, A. *Getting It Done: From Commitment to Action on Funding for Women and Girls*. New York: Women and Foundations/Corporate Philanthropy, 1992.

Bronfman, J. "The Experience of Inherited Wealth." Ann Arbor, Mich.: University Microfilms, 1987. This dissertation is available only through University Microfilms, Inc., and was one of the ten best-selling dissertations in its catalogue in 1990.

Carson, E. *The Contemporary Charitable Giving and Voluntarism of Black Women*. New York: Center for the Study of Philanthropy, City University of New York, Graduate School and University Center, 1987.

The Challenge of Being Female: A Conference on Philanthropy and Women's Issues in Southern California. Los Angeles: Los Angeles Women's Foundation, 1990.

NEW DIRECTIONS FOR PHILANTHROPIC FUNDRAISING, NO. 2, WINTER 1993 © JOSSEY-BASS PUBLISHERS

Changing the Face of Philanthropy. 1985–92 Report. St. Paul, Minn.: National Network of Women's Funds, 1993.

Coles, R. *Children of Crisis.* Vol. 5: *Privileged Ones: The Well-Off and the Rich in America.* Boston: Little, Brown, 1977.

Conway, J. K. *The Female Experience in Eighteenth- and Nineteenth-Century America.* New York: Garland, 1982.

Couturier, E. *Opulent Foundations and Women's Philanthropy in Colonial Mexico.* New York: Center for the Study of Philanthropy, City University of New York, Graduate School and University Center, 1987.

Daniels, A. K. *Invisible Careers: Women Civic Leaders from the Volunteer World.* Chicago: University of Chicago Press, 1988.

Danky, J. P. (ed.). *Women's Periodicals and Newspapers from the 18th Century to 1981.* Boston, Mass.: G. K. Hall in association with the State Historical Society of Wisconsin, 1982.

deAzevedo, C. M. *Philanthropy and Brazilian Women's Movements.* New York: Center for the Study of Philanthropy, City University of New York, Graduate School and University Center, 1987.

Directory of Women in Marquis Who's Who Publications. Wilmette, Ill.: Marquis Who's Who, 1984.

Directory of Women's Funds, 1993. Published annually. Send SASE to National Network of Women's Funds, 1821 University Avenue, Suite 409 North, St. Paul, MN 55104.

Empowering Women in Philanthropy. Los Angeles: Feminist Majority Foundation, 1991.

Fisher, J. "A Study of Six Women Philanthropists of the Early Twentieth Century." Unpublished doctoral dissertation, Graduate School of the Union Institute, Cincinnati, Ohio, 1992. Available through University Microfilms, Inc., Ann Arbor, Mich.

Galvin, K. *Far from Done: The Challenge of Diversifying Philanthropic Leadership.* New York: Women and Foundations/Corporate Philanthropy, 1990.

Gelb, J. *Feminism and Philanthropy in the United States and England.* New York: City University of New York, Center for the Study of Philanthropy, 1990.

Goodale, F. A. (ed.). *The Literature of Philanthropy.* New York: HarperCollins, 1993.

Hinding, A. *Women's History Sources: A Guide to Archives and Manuscript Collections in the United States.* New York: Bowker, 1979.

Humphreys, N. K. *American Women's Magazines: An Annotated Historical Guide.* New York: Garland, 1989.

International Who's Who in Community Service. Cambridge, England: Melrose Press, 1974 and later (irregular).

International Who's Who of Women. London: Europa Publications, 1992.

James, E. T. (ed.). *Notable American Women, 1607–1950.* 3 vols. Cambridge, Mass.: Belknap Press of Harvard University Press, 1971.

Kert, B. *Abby Aldrich Rockefeller: The Woman in the Family*. New York: Random House, 1993.

Kosmin, B. *The Political Economy of Gender in Jewish Federations*. New York: Center for the Study of Philanthropy, City University of New York, Graduate School and University Center, 1987.

Leonard, J. (ed.). *Woman's Who's Who of America, 1914–15*. New York: American Commonwealth, 1914.

Library and Information Sources on Women. New York: City University of New York, Feminist Press, 1988.

Lundberg, F. *America's 60 Families*. New York: Vanguard Press, 1937.

Lyons, L., and Wilson, J. (eds.). *Who's Who Among Women of California*. San Francisco: Security Publishing, 1922. "An Annual Devoted to the Representative Women of California with an Authoritative Review of Their Activities in Civic, Social, Athletic, Philanthropic, Art, and Music, Literary and Dramatic Circles."

McCarthy, K. *Noblesse Oblige*. Chicago: University of Chicago Press, 1982.

McCarthy, K. *Lady Bountiful Revisited*. New Brunswick, N.J.: Rutgers University Press, 1991.

McCarthy, K. *Women's Culture: American Philanthropy and Art, 1830–1930*. Chicago: University of Chicago Press, 1992.

Menschel, R. *Women as Contributors to Higher Education*. Ithaca, N.Y.: Cornell University, 1993.

Metzger, Z. (ed.). *Special Report on Women's Funds*. Washington, D.C.: National Committee for Responsive Philanthropy, 1986.

Mogil, C., and Slepian, A. *We Gave It All Away*. Philadelphia: New Society Publishers, 1992.

New York Times Cumulative Subject and Personal Name Index: Women 1965–75. Glen Rock, N.J.: Microfilming Corporation of America, 1978.

Odendahl, T. (ed.). *America's Wealthy and the Future of Foundations*. New York: Foundation Center, 1987.

Odendahl, T. *Charity Begins at Home*. New York: Basic Books, 1990.

Ostrander, S. A. *Women of the Upper Class*. Philadelphia: Temple University Press, 1984.

Ostrower, F. *Elite Insiders and Outsiders: Consequences for Philanthropy*. New Haven, Conn.: Yale University Program on Non-Profit Organizations, 1992.

Principal Women of America: Being the Biographies of Approximately One Thousand Five Hundred American Women Who Stand Pre-Eminent in Their Country. 3 vols. London: Mitre Press, 1932, 1936, 1940.

Ritacco, R. (comp.). *WAF/CP Membership Directory*. New York: Women and Foundations/Corporate Philanthropy, 1993. Available only to members. Published biennially.

Ritacco, R., and Cole, R. (comps.). *Directory of Women's Funds*. (Rev. ed.) New York: Women and Foundations/Corporate Philanthropy, 1989.

Scott, A. F. "Most Invisible of All: Black Women's Voluntary Associations." *Journal of Southern History*, 1990, *56*, 3–22.

Scott, A. F. *Natural Allies: Women's Associations in American History*. Champaign: University of Illinois Press, 1993.

Sedgwick, J. *Rich Kids*. New York: Morrow, 1985.

Sicherman, B., and Green, C. (eds.). *Notable American Women*. Vol. 4: *The Modern Period*. Cambridge, Mass.: The Belknap Press of Harvard University Press, 1980.

Smith, J. C. (ed.). *Notable Black American Women*. Detroit: Gale Research, 1991.

Stern, M. B. *We the Women: Career Firsts of Nineteenth Century America*. New York: Schulte, 1963.

Stoddard, H. *Famous American Women*. Mineola, N.Y.: Dover, 1970.

Stone, K., and Sublett, D. "The UCLA Women and Philanthropy Focus Groups Report." Unpublished report. Los Angeles: Office of Development, University of California, Los Angeles, 1992.

Telgen, D., and Kemp, J. (eds.). *Notable Hispanic American Women*. Detroit: Gale Research, 1993.

Uglow, J. S. (ed.). *International Dictionary of Women's Biography*. New York: Continuum, 1982.

Uglow, J. S. (ed.). *The Continuum Dictionary of Women's Biography*. (Expanded ed.) New York: Continuum, 1989.

Who's Who of American Women. Wilmette, Ill.: Marquis Who's Who, (annual).

Women Directors of the Top 1,000 Corporations, 1993. Washington, D.C.: The National Women's Economic Alliance Foundation, 1993. Available from 1440 New York Avenue, N.W., Suite 30, Washington, D.C. 20005. Telephone (202) 393-5257.

Women's College Coalition. *Alumnae Giving at Women's Colleges: A Ten Year Report*. Washington, D.C., 1988.

World Who's Who of Women. (11th ed.) Cambridge, England: International Biographical Centre, 1992.

Articles

Alexander, R. "At Duke, a Women's Studies Archivist." "Chronicle" column. *New York Times*, Mar. 23, 1993, p. A21. Sallie Bingham's $750,000 gift to endow the position of women's studies archivist at Duke University.

"Alumnae Associations." *Chicago Tribune*, July 25, 1993, p. 1. The establishment of the Council of 100 at Northwestern University.

Atchison, S. "Now, It's 'Sister, Can You Spare a Dime?' " *Business Week*, January 29, 1990, p. 58.

Bailey, A. L. "Creating Alliances to Combat Global Poverty." *Chronicle of Philanthropy*, June 4, 1991, p. 6. The Synergos Foundation, founded by Peggy Dulany, and its work.

Bates, K. G. "Women in Philanthropy." *Lear's*, Dec. 1989, p. 32.

Bennett, L. "Giving 'Til It Helps." *Detroit Free Press*, July 4, 1993, p. 4. Mary Jo Pulte and the establishment of the Michigan Women's Foundation.

Beyette, B. "Feminism, Philanthropy: Fighting the Funding Gap." *Los Angeles Times*, May 13, 1988, p. 5:1.

"The Billionaires . . . and Many Are Women." *Fortune*, Sept. 9, 1991, cover story.

Bingham, S. "Growing Up Rich." *Ms.*, June 1986, p. 48.

Bleakley, F. "Broker's Generosity Generates Business, Worries Wall Street." *The Wall Street Journal*, July 7, 1992, p. C1. Muriel Stebert, the first woman to own a seat on the New York Stock Exchange.

Blumenstyk, G. "New Head of Ford Fund's Education Program Is Champion of Women and Minority Students." *Chronicle of Higher Education*, Dec. 9, 1992, p. A27.

Buckley, M. L. "A Chronicle of Fair Ladies." *Harvard Today*, May 1959.

Butterfield, F. "As for That Myth About How Much Alumnae Give." *New York Times*, Feb. 26, 1992, p. B6.

Cahill, K. "The 250 Richest Women in Britain." *Business Age*, Oct. 1992, p. 1.

Calhoun, S. "New Ways to Lead." *Foundation News*, Nov./Dec. 1987, p. 24. The establishment of Women and Foundations/Corporate Philanthropy.

Churcher, S. "Making It by Doing Good." *The New York Times Sunday Magazine*, July 3, 1988, p. 16.

Curtis, C. "The Gregarious Anne Getty." *The New York Times*, Oct. 8, 1985, p. C4.

Danforth, K. "Out with a Bang." *Foundation News*, Jan./Feb. 1993, p. 22. Irene Diamond's work at the foundation she and her husband established.

Downey, M. "Women Are Starting to Open Their Checkbooks and Donate, but They Still Lag Behind Men," *Atlanta Journal and Constitution*, July 30, 1992, p. C1.

Downey, M. "Female Giving: Dollars and Some Change." *Atlanta Constitution*, July 30, 1992.

"Emily's Helping." *Chicago Tribune*, Feb. 14, 1993, *Womanews*, p. 1.

"Forum Addresses Issues Related to Women in Philanthropy." *Philanthropy Matters* (Indiana Center on Philanthropy), Fall 1992, p. 5.

Friedman, J. "The Founding Mother." *New York Times Magazine*, May 2, 1993, p. 50.

Gale, E. "Two Women's Gifts of Twenty-Five Millions." Unidentified magazine, 1900. Jane Stanford's and Phoebe Hearst's gifts to Stanford University.

Goldberg, D. "How the Other Half Gives." *CASE Currents*, Mar. 1989, p. 11.

Goss, K. "Philanthropies Aimed at Addressing Issues of Special Concern to Women Are Sprouting Rapidly." *Chronicle of Philanthropy*, Apr. 18, 1989, p. 4.

Goss, K. "Women's Funds Raised $14.8 Million in 1989." *Chronicle of Philanthropy*, Apr. 17, 1990, p. 10.

Goss, K. "Young Women Seen as Top Leaders and Backers of Social Action Causes." *Chronicle of Philanthropy*, Jan. 15, 1991, p. 21.

Goss, K. "Gifts to Women's Funds Decline." *Chronicle of Philanthropy*, May 7, 1991, p. 10.

Hall, H. "Women's New Charity Clout." *Chronicle of Philanthropy*, June 16, 1992, p. 1.

Hall, H. "Female Leaders Encourage Expanded Efforts to Increase Charitable Giving by Women." *Chronicle of Philanthropy*, Nov. 3, 1992, p. 10.

Hanna, J. "Abby Foundation Puts Its Money Behind Women." *Chicago Tribune*, Apr. 4, 1993, p. 18SW1.

Hardie, A. "Spelman Gets $37 Million Gift: Reader's Digest Founder's Bequest Is the Largest Ever to a Black College." *Atlanta Journal and Constitution*, May 6, 1992, p. A1.

Hendrix, K. "Peg Yorkin Was the Housewife of the '50s: Now, She's an Activist with Clout and Money: The $10 Million Woman." *Los Angeles Times*, Oct. 4, 1991, p. E1. Peg Yorkin's gift to the Fund for a Feminist Majority.

Henry, F. "Agnes Gund Recounts Her Blessings." *Cleveland Plain Dealer*, Nov. 16, 1992, p. 3C.

"Ideal Donor Profile Seen Altered by Populations Shifts, Competition." *Chronicle of Philanthropy*, Apr. 18, 1989, p. 10.

Johnson, R. E. "Millionairess Camille Cosby Says She Had to Earn Ph.D. Degree Because 'You Have to Do What You Urge Others to Do.'" *Jet*, June 15, 1992, p. 12.

Johnston, D. "Women Take Aim at Charity Gender Gap." *Los Angeles Times*, Aug. 1987, p. 1.

Jones, R. "Colorado's $1 Million Day." *Rocky Mountain News*, Dec. 6, 1992, p. 8.

Joseph, D. "Women's Funds Suffer a Decrease in Donations, but Endowments Show Growth." *Chronicle of Philanthropy*, Sept. 22, 1992, p. 30.

Klein, K. "Confessions of a Feminist Fund-Raiser." *Ms.*, Nov./Dec. 1991, p. 34.

Kozinn, A. "Juilliard School to Receive a $10 Million Endowment." *The New York Times*, Jan. 15, 1992, p. C15. Irene Diamond's gift for a scholarship and faculty salaries fund.

Lacy, T. "A Lesson for Women from '92." *Boston Globe*, May 3, 1993, p. 21.

"Learning to Think Big When Giving to Charity." *Cleveland Plain Dealer*, Nov. 24, 1992, p. 1C.

Lederer, L. "Funding Strategies for the Nineties." *Ms.*, Nov./Dec. 1991, p. 38.

Lee, H. "Philanthropy and the Love of Power." Review of *Beatrice Webb: Woman of Conflict,* by C. Seymour-Jones. *The Independent, Sunday Book Review,* Mar. 8, 1992, p. 26.

Lewis, D. "Grassroots Support for Women." *Boston Globe,* Nov. 16, 1992, p. 17.

"Loaded! The Twenty Richest Women in the World." *Harpers & Queen,* Mar. 1991, cover story.

Lorch, D. "Goddard Leaves $20 Million to N.Y.U." *The New York Times,* May 18, 1990, p. B1. Paulette Goddard's legacy.

McCarthy, K. "Parallel Power Structures: Women and the Voluntary Sector." Reprinted in *Giving USA Update,* Mar./Apr. 1989, p. 6.

McCarthy, R. "So Many Capable Women with Such Drive." *Atlanta Journal and Constitution,* Mar. 3, 1992, p. C6.

McCullom, R. "Women's Groups Continue to Feel Shortchanged by Grantmakers." *Donor's Forum,* July/Aug. 1990, p. 6.

McKenna, S. "Profile: Walteen Grady Truely." *Newsday,* Sept. 22, 1992, p. 26.

McMillen, L. "New Women's Funds Tend to Shun Contributions to Colleges in Favor of Support for Activist Organizations." *Chronicle of Higher Education,* Apr. 27, 1988, p. A32.

McMillen, L. "Study Finds Alumnae of Women's Colleges Give More Generously." *Chronicle of Higher Education,* Oct. 5, 1988, p. A37.

McMillen, L. "College Fund Raisers See Their Alumnae as Untapped Donors." *Chronicle of Philanthropy,* Apr. 1, 1992, p. A31.

Mason, D. "Women Take Lead in Helping Women." *St. Petersburg Times,* Apr. 25, 1992, p. A1.

Matthews, A. "Alma Maters Court Their Daughters." *New York Times Sunday Magazine,* Apr. 7, 1991, pp. 40, 42.

Meyer, M. "Take Notice." *Houston Chronicle,* Sept. 6, 1992, p. 2.

Meyeroff, W. "Purse Strings: Courting Philanthropists to Look at Charity in a Different Light." *Chicago Tribune Womanews,* Mar. 29, 1992, p. 12.

Miller, J. "Old Money, New Needs: New York's Brooke Astor." *New York Times Sunday Magazine,* Nov. 17, 1991, p. 40.

Mullinex, D. "Women in Philanthropy Forum November 17." *Indianapolis Star,* Oct. 31, 1993.

Nash, A. "Woman Who Overturned an Empire." *Ms.,* June 1986, p. 44.

Newman, L. "A Philanthropist Reaches Out for Other Philanthropists." *Chicago Tribune Womanews,* Feb. 7, 1993, p. 2. Tracy Gary and the group Chicago Women in Philanthropy.

Pa$$ It On. Quarterly newsletter. National Network of Women's Funds, Minneapolis, Minn.

"Philanthropies Aimed at Addressing Issues of Special Concern to Women Are Sprouting Rapidly." *Chronicle of Philanthropy,* Apr. 18, 1989, p. 4.

Pogrebin, L. C. "Contributing to the Cause." *The New York Times Sunday Magazine,* Apr. 22, 1990, p. 22.

"The Power of Money." *Radcliffe Quarterly*, Dec. 1991, p. 2.

Richman, R. "Special Gifts: Women Put Their Money Where It Really Counts." *Chicago Tribune*, Dec. 13, 1992, p. 6:1.

Rohan, V. "Control, Women, and Money: The Cookie Jar or the Portfolio?" *Smith College Quarterly*, Spring 1986, p. 28.

Schneider, S. W. "Jewish Women's Philanthropy." First of a two-part series. *Lilith*, Winter 1993, p. 6. Second part will be published in 1994.

Shaw, S., and Taylor, M. "Career Women: A Changing Environment for Philanthropy." *National Society of Fund Raising Executives Journal*, Fall 1991, p. 43.

Spiegel, I. "Women's Role Cited in Jewish Agencies That Raise Funds." *The New York Times*, Nov. 24, 1975, p. 53.

Steinem, G. "The Trouble with Rich Women." *Ms.*, June 1986, p. 41.

Tabankin, M. "No Fund Raising Favors for Women." *The New York Times*, Apr. 10, 1993, p. 19.

Tanner, N. N. "Single Sex Education and Fund Raising: Why Have Women's Colleges Been So Successful?" *Women's Philanthropy* (newsletter of the National Network on Women as Philanthropists), Fall 1992, p. 1.

Teltsch, K. "Philanthropist Recalls the Joy of Giving over 50 Years." *The New York Times*, June 12, 1983, p. A65. Lucy Goldschmidt Moses's philanthropy.

Teltsch, K. "The Incognito Fund: A Source of Silent Generosity." *The New York Times*, Sept. 23, 1984, p. 50.

Teltsch, K. "Philanthropy: Women Appeal." *The New York Times*, May 17, 1985, p. 36.

Teltsch, K. "Network of Women Hopes to Change American Philanthropy." *The New York Times*, May 14, 1986, p. C7.

Teltsch, K. "At Foundations, the Voice of Women and Minorities Remains Faint." *The New York Times*, Apr. 7, 1990, p. A9.

Teltsch, K. "$1 Million to Endow Star Chair." *The New York Times*, Mar. 27, 1991, p. B7. Joanne Woodward's establishment of a professorship in public policy at Sarah Lawrence College.

Teltsch, K. "$170 Million Legacy, the Bulk of an Estate, Goes to Charity." *The New York Times*, Mar. 28, 1991, p. B6. Lucy Goldschmidt Moses's bequests.

Teltsch, K. "$37 Million Windfall for Black Women's College." *The New York Times*, May 6, 1992, p. B15. Gift from the DeWitt Wallace/Spelman College Fund established by the founder of *Reader's Digest*.

Teltsch, K. "A New Leader for a Foundation That Aids Women." "Chronicle" column. *The New York Times*, Aug. 31, 1992, p. B4. Walteen Grady Truely's appointment as head of Women and Foundations/Corporate Philanthropy.

Teltsch, K. "Shaking Up Old Ways of Benevolence." *The New York Times*, Sept. 15, 1992, p. B1.

Temin, C. "Heiress Finds Philanthropy Not Always Easy." *Boston Globe*, Feb. 23, 1985, p. 21. Charlene Engelhard and the Engelhard Foundation.

Thompson, A., and Kaminski, A. "Women's Philanthropy No Longer Invisible." *Wingspread Journal*, Winter 1993, p. 3.

Thompson, C. "Donors Skirt Issue When It Comes to Funding Women's Aid Agencies." *Chicago Tribune*, Nov. 18, 1992, p. 2C4.

Vitale, S. "Beyond the Bake Sale." *Savvy*, 1990, p. 13.

Vobejda, B. "Cosbys Donate $20 Million to Atlanta's Spelman College; Many Black Institutions Suffering Financially." *Washington Post*, Nov. 9, 1988, p. 95.

White, D. "A Network of Networks: A Global Fund for Women Uses the Process and Product of Grantmaking to Improve the Lives of Half the Population." *Foundation News*, Jan./Feb. 1993, p. 26.

Whitney, R. "Putting Our Money Where Our Mouth Is." *Glamour*, June 1992, p. 116.

Williams, L. S. "Making a Way Out of No Way: Black Women's Clubs and Philanthropy 1900–1940." Paper delivered at the Conference on Philanthropy in the African-American Experience, Rockefeller Archives Center, Sept. 1992.

Yarrow, A. "Feminist Philanthropy Comes into Its Own." *The New York Times*, May 21, 1983, p. A7.

Zehr, M. A. "Look Deeper into Indian Country: Native American Women Challenge Foundations to Think Harder About How They Fund American Indian Issues." *Foundation News*, Sept./Oct. 1993, p. 12.

Research libraries and other sources

The Archives and Sophia Smith Collection at Smith College: Sherrill Redmon, Director, Alumnae Gymnasium, Smith College, Northampton, MA 01063. Telephone (413) 585-2970.

The Arthur and Elizabeth Schlesinger Library on the History of Women in America: Pat King, Director, 10 Garden Street, Cambridge, MA 02138. Telephone (617) 495-8647.

Center for the Study of Philanthropy: Kathleen McCarthy, Director, Graduate School and University Center, City University of New York, 33 West 42nd Street, Room 1525, New York, NY 10036. Telephone (212) 642-2130.

Center for the Study of Research on Women: Susan Bailey, Director, Wellesley College, 106 Central Street, Wellesley, MA 02181. Telephone (617) 283-2500.

Center for the Study of Women and Philanthropy: School of Family Resources, University of Wisconsin, 1300 Linden Drive, Madison, WI 53708. Telephone (608) 263-5762.

Center for Women's Global Leadership at Rutgers University/Douglas College: PO Box 270, New Brunswick, NJ 08903. Telephone (908) 932-8782.

Feminist Majority Foundation: Eleanor Smeal, President, 1600 Wilson Boulevard, Suite 801, Arlington, VA 22209. Telephone (703) 522-2214.

The Impact Project: Anne Slepian (co-author of *We Gave It All Away*), 21 Linwood Street, Arlington, MA 02174. Telephone (617) 648-0776. This group is similar in mission to Resourceful Women in California.

Indiana Center on Philanthropy Forum on Women in Philanthropy: Melissa Brown or Paul Parker-Sawyers, 550 West North Street, Suite 301, Indianapolis, IN 46202. Telephone (317) 274-4200.

Institute for Research on Women and Gender at Stanford University: Iris Litt, Director, Serra House, Stanford, CA 94305. Telephone (415) 723-1994.

Investing in Women (newsletter): Ms. Foundation for Women, 141 Fifth Avenue, 6S, New York, NY 10001. Telephone (212) 353-8580.

Ms. Foundation for Women: Marie Wilson, President, Robin Rosenbluth, Director of Development, 141 Fifth Avenue, 6S, New York, NY 10001. Telephone (212) 353-8580.

National Council for Research on Women: Mary Ellen Capek, Executive Director, 47–49 East 65th Street, New York, NY 10021. Telephone (212) 274-0730.

National Network of Women as Philanthropists: Martha Taylor and Sondra Shaw, Directors, 1300 Linden Drive, Madison, WI 53706. Telephone (608) 262-1962; Fax (608) 262-5335.

National Network of Women's Funds: Carol Mollner, Executive Director, 1821 University Avenue, Suite 409, North St. Paul, MN 55104. Telephone (612) 641-0742.

Program on Women and Philanthropy at the University of California, Los Angeles, Development Office: Dyan Sublett and Karen Stone, Directors, 405 Hilgard Avenue, Los Angeles, CA 90024-1359. Telephone (310) 206-0614.

University of Michigan Task Force on Increasing Women's Involvement in Development at the University of Michigan: Mallory Simpson, Director of Corporations and Foundations, University of Michigan Office of Development, 301 East Liberty, Ann Arbor, MI 48104. Telephone (313) 998-6070.

Wealth of Possibilities (newsletter): Chela Blitt and Mary James, Editors, Women Donors Network/Resourceful Women, 3543 18th Street, #9, San Francisco, CA 94110. Telephone (415) 431-5677.

Women and Foundations/Corporate Philanthropy: Walteen Grady Truely, President, 322 Eighth Avenue, Room 702, New York, NY 10001. Telephone (212) 463-9934. WAF/CP issues annual reports and publishes a newsletter.

Women Donors Network/Resourceful Women: Tracy Gary, Executive Director, 3543 18th Street, #9, San Francisco, CA 94110. Telephone (415)

431-5677. "A national membership organization open to globally active women donors who are giving at least $25,000 annually to social change and social justice philanthropy."

Women's College Coalition, Jadwiga Sebrechts, Executive Director, 1090 Vermont Avenue, N.W., 3rd Floor, Washington, D.C. 20005. Telephone (202) 789-2556.

Women's Philanthropy (newsletter): National Network of Women as Philanthropists, 1300 Linden Drive, Madison, WI 53706. Telephone (608) 262-1962; Fax (608) 262-5335.

Index

92, 113; Jewish, 137–139; learning about, 79–82; motivations of, 6–8, 16, 51–55, 69, 80, 131, 141; need for research on, 18–19, 135–136; new emphasis on, 5, 61, 73–74, 85–86, 99–100, 109–111, 114–115, 132, 135; older, 29; and pledging, 129; to political action committee, 109–113; stereotypes of, 58–59, 120, 124; targeting, 28, 61; targeting, in coeducational institutions, 73–83; targeting segments among, 62–72, 112, 114; values of, 29, 113; as volunteer solicitors, 86–95, 123–124, 129; wealthy, 8, 16, 19, 54–55, 58, 114, 138–139; and women's funds, 17–18

Women donors program, in coeducational university: direction and goals for, 78–79; market research for, 79–82; publicity for, 82; resources for, 79; and women's collegiate involvement, 76–77

Women of color, giving patterns of, 11–13, 14

Women political candidates, 107–109

Women's colleges: capital campaign for, 119–133; culture of, 118–119; direct-mail message specification model for, 61–72; fundraising success of, 6–8, 117–118. See also Capital campaign; Colleges/universities

Women's Foundation, 98

Women's funds, 17–18; characteristics of, 100; decision making in, 101, 103; definition of, 98; extent of, 97, 98; goals and structure of, 100–105; opportunities for women in, 100–101; policy issues in, 102; pressures in, 104; reasons for growth of, 99–100

Women's issues, fundraising for, 103

Women's magazines, 23, 26, 141

Women's Way, 98

Woolf, V., 58, 59

Yeakel, L., 108

Yorkin, P., 59

You Just Don't Understand (Tannen), 36

Young & Rubicam, 23

Zinn, L., 23, 32

Ordering Information

NEW DIRECTIONS FOR PHILANTHROPIC FUNDRAISING is published quarterly in Fall, Winter, Spring, and Summer and available for purchase by subscription and individually.

SUBSCRIPTIONS for 1993–94 cost $59.00 for individuals (a savings of 35 percent over single-copy prices) and $79.00 for institutions, agencies, and libraries. Please do not send institutional checks for personal subscriptions. Standing orders are accepted.

SINGLE COPIES cost $19.95 when payment accompanies order. (California, New Jersey, New York, and Washington, D.C., residents please include appropriate sales tax.) Billed orders will be charged postage and handling.

DISCOUNTS for quantity orders are available. Please write to the address below for information.

ALL ORDERS must include either the name of an individual or an official purchase order number. Please submit your order as follows:
  Subscriptions: specify series and year subscription is to begin
  Single copies: include individual title code (such as PF1)

MAIL ALL ORDERS TO:
  Jossey-Bass Publishers
  350 Sansome Street
  San Francisco, California 94104-1310

FOR SINGLE-COPY SALES OUTSIDE OF THE UNITED STATES CONTACT:
  Maxwell Macmillan International Publishing Group
  866 Third Avenue
  New York, New York 10022-6221

FOR SUBSCRIPTION SALES OUTSIDE OF THE UNITED STATES, contact any international subscription agency or Jossey-Bass directly.